THE
THIRD FLOOR
MOVIE MYSTERY

DANIEL MCTEIGUE

authorHOUSE®

AuthorHouse™
1663 Liberty Drive
Bloomington, IN 47403
www.authorhouse.com
Phone: 1-800-839-8640

Published by AuthorHouse 11/20/2014

ISBN: 978-1-4969-3138-2 (sc)
ISBN: 978-1-4969-3139-9 (e)

CONTENTS

I am thankful to my Mother for her financial support to get this project going. I am also thankful that she believed in the idea of the book even though it was strange. She pretty much told me to "go for it." Thanks Mom. You're the Greatest!

I must give thanks to the artist I found by way of searching. I am thankful to the Gods that I was lead to her. Amanda Banaszewski did a great job of listening to what I wanted done and was very professional. She was proactive in that she gave me some ideas of which some were used. I was lucky to find an artist with such excellent skills.

Amanda Banaszewski, a South -Eastern Pennsylvanian multi-media artist holding a BFA from Arcadia University, who is currently focusing on urban landscapes and portraits of the odd, worked in sync with Author Dan McTeigue's direction to create this night-scene cover through digital manipulation of the original Pen and Ink Illustration.

Amanda Banaszewski
Multi-Media Freelance Artist
Contact: moonlightmaelstrom@hotmail.com

I also have to give thanks to Donna Taft at Author House Publishing for all of the help she gave me along the way.

I would like to thank all of the nice people at Author House Publishing for all of their help. As a new author I knew nothing about how to put a book together. Author House was so proactive, supportive and professional they made me feel like a pro. I was surprised by their level of attention.

I have to give thanks to the movie website called TMDb. Its full name is The Movie Database dot org. I found the release date and the movie stars on this wonderful website. If you've never heard of The Movie Database you've got to go check it out. If you're a fan of cinema you've got to put TMDb on your favorites. Thank you TMDb!

FOOTNOTES

LIVING ON LUCK: SELECTED LETTERS 1960S-1970S VOLUME 2 BY CHARLES BUKOWSKI, EDITED BY SEAMUS COONEY, COPYRIGHT 1995, HARPERCOLLINS PUBLISHERS (8*)

SCREAMS FROM THE BALCONY: SELECTED LETTERS 1960-1970 BY CHARLES BUKOWSKI, EDITED BY SEAMUS COONEY, COPYRIGHT 1978, HARPERCOLLINS PUBLISHERS (3*, 4*, 5*)

SOUTH OF NO NORTH BY CHARLES BUKOWSKI, COPYRIGHT 1973, HARPERCOLLINS PUBLISHERS (12*)

LAST NIGHT OF THE EARTH POEMS BY CHARLES BUKOWSKI, COPYRIGHT 1992, HARPERCOLLINS PUBLISHERS (11*)

PORTIONS OF A WINE STAINED NOTEBOOK BY CHARLES BUKOWSKI, COPYRIGHT 2008, REPRINTED BY PERMISSION OF CITY LIGHTS BOOKS (4 QUOTES) (2*, 6*, 7*, 9*)

BUKOWSKI: A LIFE BY NEELI CHERVOSKI, COPYRIGHT 1991, 1997, STEERFORTH PRESS (10*)

THE PLEASURES OF THE DAMNED: POEMS 1951-1993 BY CHARLES BUKOWSKI, COPYRIGHT 2007, HARPERCOLLINS PUBLISHERS (1*)

CHAPTER ONE
INTRODUCTION

This book is about a discovery I made whereby I started to notice a surprisingly large number of times that the phrase Third Floor was mentioned in movies. I decided one day to start writing down each time I heard or saw Third Floor being mentioned in movies, and then later in TV shows as well. This book is only going to be focused on movies. The reason I was drawn to or heard the phrase Third Floor so readily was because I was once in a rock 'n roll band called Third Floor. I had the phrase or the title Third Floor emblazoned across my brain. We were together for 2 ¼ years and we played a lot of the bars and clubs in the Philly suburbs and a few of the totally cool, legendary places on Philadelphia's popular South Street.

This book is about examining the mystery of why the phrase Third Floor appears in so many movies and also in a lot of TV shows as well. I felt like, "What the heck is going on here?" I am curious about this phenomenon, I really am. I hope I can draw you, the reader, into this mystery as well.

This whole process began when I first watched the movie, "Barfly", written by Charles Bukowski and directed by Barbet Schroeder. I remember thinking that the movie was really creepy. It was being shown on Showtime and it had been released in the fall of 1987 and VCRs were a recent new invention and I owned one. I was amazed that I could tape any big name blockbuster movie and that I could watch it whenever I wanted to. This was a sea change in how people could view movies. I went a little nuts, like a lot of people did, and I started to record a lot of different things, like NFL playoff football games for instance. For the most part though I recorded movies.

Since I had recorded "Barfly" I could watch it whenever I wanted to. They had stopped showing it on Showtime but that didn't matter anymore because I had it on tape. The movie grew on me. I started to love the character of Henry Chinaski. He was a bad alcoholic who lived close to skid row. He was a poet though and he was a good poet at that. He was involved with an ongoing battle with a night bartender and they used to beat the crap out of each other in the back alley. The fight scenes were bloody, dark, very violent, and in a way heartbreaking. Our character, Henry, sure could take a beating.

As the months went by I found myself drawn to the movie especially if I was going to drink beer or if I had already had a few. I started to remember the few lines of poetry spoken. It was not like any kind of poetry I had ever heard before. The movie was growing on me. I asked people at work if they knew about the movie. Very few of them heard of it and the few people who did, said they really didn't like it very much. This movie definitely was not a blockbuster type movie. It looked like "Barfly" was destined to become one of those underground or cult movies. At this time I never really thought about learning more about the real poet. I was the sort of person who could care less about poetry, in fact I kind of hated poetry. I was busy working full time and trying to put bands together so I could jam. I was obsessed with drumming and working on original music. It would be several more years before I started to learn more about the real Charles Bukowski.

There is one particular scene in the "Barfly" where our main character Henry Chinaski meets this woman in a bar at night. They leave the bar together and stop off at a liquor store to get alcohol, cigars, and cigarettes. As they are walking on the sidewalk at night she says. "My place is next. I'm up on the Third Floor." As they continue on the way to the woman's apartment they pass by a small mound of land and on the top of this mound is corn. The woman, whose name was Wanda Wilcox decides she has to have some of this corn. The corn is still green and it has not grown enough to be edible. Henry yells at Wanda from the sidewalk down below, "Hey wait you can't go up there. You'll be seen." She doesn't stop gathering the corn. She is shoving some ears into her purse. Henry yells up to her, "Hey, hey what are you doing?" Henry reasons that the cops could see her up there.

Sure enough the cops show up and they are shouting on their megaphone to stop, to freeze. But, our main character friends are running full speed towards Wanda's building. They run to the basement entrance with the cops shining a light on them. Even though my band "Third Floor" hadn't yet come to be, I remembered that line she said about living on the Third Floor.

This book is an investigation, exploration, and documentation of the mystery of the prevalence of the phrase "Third Floor" in so many movies. I am incredibly curious as to the origin of this phenomenon. Is this just a coincidence? No way! It occurs too many times. Is there some sort of conspiracy among writers to use this phrase consistently? But why would they do that? At this point you may be thinking, "Who gives a damn." Or you may be saying, "What difference does it make." These are valid points but for me it was something that unfolded very slowly. Year after year I heard this phrase in movie after movie. Sometimes the words Third Floor aren't spoken but instead there will be a scene that takes place on the Third Floor or there will be a large number three painted on a wall while there is a scene going on in a parking garage or an outdoor stairwell for instance. There is one movie where an elevator malfunctions and it finally crashes on the Third Floor. Why does it crash on the Third Floor? Why doesn't it crash on the fourth floor or the fifth floor?

If you are a fan of cinema and you like your TV shows as well this book is for you. As I had mentioned before this book is going to focus on movies but the Third Floor phenomenon is present in TV shows as well. You can keep an eye out for it. You can join in on the mystery. As you watch a movie don't be surprised to see that your favorite character lives in apartment 306 or may be apartment 3B. I have included all apartments or doctors offices or secret hideouts that have a 300 series number. The way I figure it is that most apartments with the 300 number on the door are on the Third Floor. I started noticing a lot of 300 series numbers so I added this to my growing list. I guess I'm going to have to set up a website so that we all have a place to document our ongoing observations.

Chapter Two
YOUTH

When I was a young boy in the 1960s I loved music like crazy. Music from the 1950's and 1960's was played on the radio and performances could be seen on TV. I was born in 1962. When I was three or four my father used to play his organ in the living room. I have some vague memories that appeared out of nowhere where my older brothers, sister, and Mom are all standing around my dad while he's playing the organ and everyone was singing. They were singing Christmas songs. So it is safe to say that I come from a musical family. My brother Pat took years of piano lessons when he was a kid. He was the firstborn child and I am the lastborn child. My other three brothers at one point in their lives all played acceptable guitar. My brother Hughie worked very hard for many years and advanced to a high level of skill as a classical guitar player. It makes me so sad that none of us had the foresight to record him playing that well. My brother Kenny could play rhythm guitar but could never get it together to play lead. My brother Marty was also good at playing guitar and singing while playing Christian praise songs when he was in his 20's and 30's. My brother Kenny also played the drums for a number of years. It was his drums that I banged on when I was a little kid. My sister Kathy, when she was a little girl, took dance lessons. She could always sing along with the radio really well when she was in her 20's. My mom has always been a really good hummer. She could hum along with every song on the radio. Just recently my sister Kathy told me that when my mom was young, in her teenage years, she could really sing. I didn't know anything about that. As you can see I'm from a musical family and the love of music runs through my veins.

All the people from my generation and my older brothers, sister, and parents and all the people across the country used to watch the Ed Sullivan show. It was on Sunday nights. Ed had on all of the best talent you could imagine. It wasn't just musicians. It was a variety show and you never knew what you were going to see. I loved that show tremendously. Everyone loved that show. My favorites were always the musicians. It was fascinating to see how each band cared so much about the songs that they were playing, that they created. Each band had their own energy and power of expression. The list of talent that was on the Ed Sullivan show is absolutely incredible. I'll list some of the big names off the top of my head: The Beatles, The Rolling Stones, The Doors, Elvis Presley, Frank Sinatra, Dean Martin, Sammy Davis Jr., The Mamas and the Papas, The Turtles, The Zombies, The Kinks, Gerry and the Pacemakers, The Dave Clark Five, The Animals, "Peter, Paul, & Mary", Anthony Newley, Ella Fitzgerald, Diana Ross and the Supremes and Bobby Darin with Mack the Knife. The list could go on and on and on.

When I used to watch the Ed Sullivan show and other shows where they showed how happy people got or when they showed a hall of people dancing and everyone appeared to be genuinely happy, I decided that I wanted to be in a band where we could make people dance and be happy. I remember lying on my stomach on the floor wearing warm flannel pajamas with the built in "footies" to keep your feet warm while watching the Ed Sullivan show. We had a fireplace and it was near the TV. I have some really fond memories of watching the Ed Sullivan show with my family members sitting around. As a kid I could sense that there was so much pain and suffering in the world and that it would be a great gift to people to help them forget all of their worries, even if only for short time while they were out there dancing and smiling. I know that sounds corny but I really wanted to do this. I wanted to be in a band that played great music and helped people go out and have a good time.

While I was watching that show I knew what I wanted to do when I grew up and that was to be a musician. I am sure that Ed Sullivan's show caused millions of little girls and boys to dream of becoming musicians. There is no doubt in my mind. In fact I talked to numerous musicians who I met in my 20s who agreed that it was from watching the Ed Sullivan show that they got hooked on rock 'n roll and wanted to be able to play in a band when they grew up.

For me it ended up being the drums. There were drums in the basement at some point during my childhood and they were my brother Kenny's. My brother Kenny had a band that jammed in our basement. There was also a guitar or two lying around the house as well. I could pick up the guitars and play them whenever I wanted. Trying to play the guitar was impossible. I could strum a little bit but trying to put my fingers on the fret board and hold my fingers down was painful beyond belief. I had no idea how anybody could do that. I was way too young to realize that if you played enough you would form hard calluses on the tips of your fingers. Look at any guitar player's fingertips and you'll see thick callus.

Lucky for me the drums were there. I could bang away on the drums and not experience pain so I stuck with the drums. I loved the fact that they were so loud. I was a little kid and I was in Catholic school, which was like being in jail. You couldn't so much as make a peep without having a Nun crack a yardstick across your skull. For me to be able to sit down at my brother's drums and make an absolute racket was a total blast. I couldn't get enough of hitting those cymbals and producing that crashing metallic sound. I was so short that I couldn't sit on the drum throne, that's what they call it. They don't call it a stool. So I had two ways of playing and exploring. First I would sit on the throne but this meant my feet couldn't touch the pedals. So, I would focus on the snare drum and the high hat. I could also hit the one tom-tom and the big floor tom, as well as one ride symbol and one crash cymbal. I just focused on all the different sounds these things made and I would try to make a beat with the snare and high hat and then tried to hit one of the cymbals in perfect beat. I was very young and my muscles were not used to this sort of thing at all. After doing that for a while, say perhaps 45 minutes I would get off of the throne and push the thrown out of the way and put my right foot on the bass drum. I would get a very strong beat going between just the bass drum and the snare drum. I was able to get very strong primal beat going in this way. I was able to learn about off beat shots on the snare while doing this. Once in a while I would try to hit a tom-tom while keeping the beat solid. I would almost get to the point where I was dancing out a beat with my whole body moving. It was really primal and I loved it. Inevitably I would do something wrong and lose the whole rhythm but this is what drumming is all about. I love playing the drums and eventually while we still had the drums my legs grew a little bit and my brother Kenny showed me how to lower the throne and I was able to try to play the proper way with both feet on the pedals. Needless to say it was incredibly complicated and it was a very frustrating endeavor. There were times I wondered who I was fooling. There are always times when you want to give up but you remember how much you just love hitting the drums and you work through little problems. An old college friend and roommate of mine once wrote a song called "Little Victories" and that is what I would have as I played those drums in our old Galloway Avenue basement in Roslyn, PA. When I look back on those days I realize I must have been playing pretty loud because the only way my mom could get my attention was by flicking the basement lights. When I saw the lights flickering off and on I knew it was dinnertime.

There was one other event that absolutely cemented my love of the drums and my total 100% conviction that I was one day going to be a drummer in a band. It was summer time in the 1960's and I was probably 8 years old so technically it was 1970 but the 60's vibe was still heavy in the air. I was at a carnival at Roslyn Elementary School. It was your typical carnival or fair with all sorts of corny races for the kids and adults who wanted to act like kids again. They had the three-legged race whereby two people stand side-by-side and their right leg is tied to the other persons left leg so that now the two people have three legs. There was the burlap sack bounce race for lack of a better term whereby you get your legs inside a burlap sack and everybody jumps up and down to the finish line to see who wins. They surely don't have carnivals like that around here anymore. Since I was a kid I participated in these events simply because they were there. But, when I heard a band starting to play I ran over there immediately. I got right up against the front of the stage and the band was pretty good. One of the songs they played was "White Room" by Cream and they played it very well. I was enraptured. My whole body was aglow with a humming joy. The music was so loud and it made me feel like a giant. These four guys on the stage were like gods to me. I watched each one of them in disbelief that they were here at this corny fair and they were playing music this well. I stared and stared at the drummer as he got those spots in the song that featured the drummer and I knew to the core of my being that that was what I wanted to do when I grew up. I am eternally grateful for those guys that day who played loud rock 'n roll music at the fair.

The drums that I got to play on in my basement were blue sparkle and they were Ludwig. It seems like all of the drums back then were Ludwig. My mom started telling me that Kenny was thinking about selling the drums. I thought to myself that that would never happen because I enjoyed playing the drums too much. No one would ever hurt my feelings that bad. No way. I told Kenny that he could never sell the drums. I loved them too much. One day I came home and ran down the basement to get ready to play and they were gone. I stood motionless, staring. I couldn't believe it.

CHAPTER THREE

JR. HIGH SCHOOL YEARS

My parents separated in the fall of 1972. I was in 5th grade. We moved to Lansdale and lived at Wissahickon Park Apartments. We lived in D building in Apt. D-308. My dad was an alcoholic. He smoked a pack and a half a day. His beer was Schaeffer and his smokes were Salem, menthol. When he was sober he was meek and mild mannered. He was pretty quiet and didn't bring a lot of attention to himself. When he was drunk he was a loud mouth and a big boaster of all his heroic attributes. He fought in World War II like so many men of his generation. It almost seemed as a kid growing up in the 1960s and 1970s that more people fought in the war then people who didn't fight in the war. My dad was a sergeant and he was a D-Day plus one guy. That meant he landed on D-Day one day after that brutally murderous bloody gory and hideous day. He was just one guy in the biggest landing of men and material in the history of this Earth up to that point and beyond that point, to this day. What it must have been like for each man in his own individual way, to view a global war. God knows what horrors my dad saw on his way through France and into Germany as part of an anti-aircraft battalion called the "Maverick Battalion." They were called so, because they moved from unit to unit so much. There is no doubt in my mind that my dad was mentally and emotionally scarred by his experience in the war, to end all wars.

My mom left my dad because she couldn't take his drinking and shouting and horrible stories about the war. He would tell such horrible stories that my mom would start crying and if I saw my mom crying, I would start crying. Some nights I couldn't wait for him to either pass out at the kitchen table or fall asleep there. I also couldn't take it anymore and I agreed with my mom that we should move away. I knew it would be painful but we had to do it. Being yanked out of my neighborhood and being dropped into some other town was traumatic for me. I went through a really ugly transition half way through fifth grade, which was the year we moved. I had a really hard time fitting in at a new school and the kids there made it hell for me. I was getting really bad grades and I was getting into fights. I had bright orange, unruly hair. People called, "carrot top," about 10,000,000 times. Luckily for me I always had a radio at my disposal when I got home. Music for me, as it has been for so many people on Earth, was a saving grace. I listened to music constantly when I was not in school. When I was in school it was very easy for me to play whole songs in my head. I had loads of songs stored up in that brain of mine. I got in trouble so many times for tapping my fingers it's ridiculous.

I wasn't going to add this information about my Jr. High sports activities but after thinking about it I have decided to add this information because it is pretty remarkable. I went to Penndale Jr. High School. We were Vikings and our colors were Purple and White. This was long before the term Middle School was invented. In the spring of 7th grade my best friend Shanney and I stood in a 2nd floor stairwell of our school and watched a whole bunch of kids running around on the outdoor track and surrounding areas within the stadium area. We watched and we knew that we could never belong there because we were not special enough. We were kind of lower middle class kids and we figured that you had to be special to be out there. We were really middle class kids. On another day we went down and stood at the fence and watched. Neither one of us spoke, we just stared. Then we started to see some of our friends. We couldn't believe it. What were they doing out there? Tizzy and someone else came over and asked what we were doing. We said we were watching. Tizzy said why don't you come in and try out. We said, "No way, we don't know what to do." Tizzy proceeded to remind us that we were two of the fastest kids around and that all's track is, running fast. Shanney and I still weren't buying it and we left. But as we were walking home we both started to realize that Tizzy was right and that we were both burners. We decided we would stick together and that we would try out. My God, low self-esteem can be a real killer. We both made the team and proceeded to run in the 440 yard relay and 75 yard and 100 yard sprints.

The 440 relay is where 4 guys run ¼ of the length of the track extremely quickly. You hand the baton to the next guy and races are pretty much won and lost during the hand off. We were coached really well and we were flawless but it took tons of practice. We won track meet after track meet. I won races in the 75 and 100 yard dashes and our 440 relay team won a lot of races as well. From what I remember I didn't run the 100 yard race the whole season. My best time in the 75 yard dash was 9.7 seconds and my best time in the 100 yard dash was 13.1 seconds. I was really fast for a red headed Irish kid. Our whole track team made it into the final matches, the playoffs essentially, and we won the whole shooting match. We were the Bucks / Mont Champs. This meant that we were the best Jr. High School in all of Bucks and Montgomery Counties. Not too shabby! It was overwhelming to me to be part of something that felt huge and was so important. Look at it this way; I was just a teeny tiny 6th grader a year before.

The next fall, which had me in 8th grade I joined the soccer team. I made the team and proceeded to be brutally tortured by the coaches. Our coaches were Mr. Landesh, who was a very good soccer player, and Mr. Siebouch, who had muscles head to toe. We did far more running in soccer than we did in track if you could try to imagine such a thing. We were eliminated in the first round of the playoffs if my memory serves me correctly. I know we made the playoffs but I am not sure when we were eliminated.

The next spring all of my track and field teammates went back out to the track so our two coaches could torture us in morbid ways. Our two coaches were Mr. Shonker who was the most intense guy you could ever meet, and Mr. Cunneham who taught English and was super mellow. They had the whole good cop, bad cop thing going on. We were too young to know about that sneaky trick. Mr Shonker taught Gym class. The pain and suffering continued but we knew that we had a great team with excellent coaches and that if we did what we did last year we might win a championship again. This will give you an idea of how badly we were worked by our coaches. In the first two weeks of the season your body is not used to that kind of torture. Even though we were skinny little healthy as all hell kids we ended up stiff as boards from the intense workouts. The other track kids and I were unable to get to class on time between classes. Our legs were so stiff it was almost impossible to get out of your chair. Then you had to hobble all the way to your next class and if it was a little bit far you would never make it. I was late to my first two classes and the second teacher gave me detention. It turned out that loads of us track kids were getting detention because we were all getting to class late. So you know what Mr. Shonker did? He ran around the building during class yelling in the classrooms to all of the teachers to not give his track kids detention. I was sitting in class and he popped his head into my class and yelled to see if any track kids were there. I raised my hand because I couldn't stand and told the teacher not to give me detention. I remember it like it was yesterday. I will love coach Shonker to the day I die.

I can still remember some of the names of the older kids. There was Bill Berker, Jeff Irish and Paul Matuskel. There the only guys I can remember. All 3 of those guys could run like the wind. They were all older kids. Well guess what folks. My little friends and I on the 440 relay team were unbeatable. We were flawless with the baton exchange and we were all very fast runners. We won at meet after meet. Other schools we faced had heard somehow that we were undefeated. That news made them want to defeat us even more. We felt the pressure week after week but we continued to win. On the last meet of the regular season we beat yet another school and went undefeated for the season at the 440 yard relay. Coach Shonker used to call us the "Mighty Mights" and we were. The guys on the relay were Tizzy, Shanney, Kerbell, and I. I also have to mention a Chinese American guy named John Wee who was on the team and week after week coach made us race to see who would be on the relay team. I had to earn my spot every week. It was torture! Poor John Wee never beat any one of us in those races but he usually lost by a nose and I'm not kidding. I wanted to kill John Wee for pushing us so hard but it was because of him breathing down our necks every week that we were so fast. After many, many weeks of this, my heart started to break for him because he was such a nice guy and he was lean muscle from head to toe but none of us wanted to give up our spots on the relay team. I know that he competed in different events on the team but I don't remember what they were. So at least he did contribute in his own way at other events.

So once again we are in the finals and we are at Central Bucks West and it's us against them. They had an extremely good team. After my events were over my friends and I walked around and watched the Javelin toss, high jumpers, long jumpers, shot put, and the brave people who did the pole vault. Apparently both teams were neck and neck all day. You are not going to believe this but the whole day came down to the last race. It was the 440 relay for the bigger guys. Bill Berker had the last leg of the race. Can you believe the whole day came down to this last race? I felt like I was gonna die. When Bill got the baton he was about 3 feet behind the guy from the other team. Keep in mind that they put their best guy on the last leg as well. Well, I haven't told you much about Bill Berker except that he looked a Greek God. He could have been on the cover of Sports Illustrated and he was a person who could probably do any sport. Everybody looked up to Bill. We figured that the race was over because you can't make up a few feet when you only have a ¼ of the track to run. Everybody from both schools were watching the two guys run. Every single person was screaming, "**GO!**" It was nerve racking. Bill started to dig in deep. He did not want to lose. He knew the whole season was riding on this last leg. And then it happened. His face turned a bright red that you could see from 40 yards away. I bet more then anything he didn't want to let coach Shonker down. It seemed to happen in slow motion but ever so slowly he started to gain on the other guy. But in the next milli second it didn't look like he gained ground at all. When it looked like it wasn't going to happen and while both runners were still in the turn before the straight away you could see it for sure, he was catching up to him. He caught him and was side by side as they went into the straightaway. Every single person in the stadium was screaming at the top of their lungs. As they went down the straightaway they were neck in neck. It was the most painful torture you could imagine; two runners who held the whole season of each team in their hands. Each runner digging deeper into their beings then either one should ever have to dig. When they got to the finish line Bill leaned to beat him at the tape. I swear to you for a brief second there was no sound and then our side went crazy and their side had to deal with crushing defeat. Crushing, crushing defeat.

My god do you want to talk about a moment you will never forget. We celebrated like we were invincible but we also had profound respect for our competitors. Since I was a year older I could understand the meaning of it all a lot better. I understood more about how big each county was and how many schools were involved. Winning a Championship like that puts you on cloud 9 for weeks. It makes life feel enjoyable for a change. I am sure Central Bucks West went on to win many Track and Field titles over the years. No one has to feel sorry for Central Buck because they proceeded to have a Football team that murdered everybody for a decade.

When the fall rolled around I got on the soccer team again and so now I'm in the 9th grade and the torture resumed where it left off. We were all better players from the year before and we jelled much more as a team. We made it into the playoffs and advanced. We ended up facing the same team that had defeated us the year before. It's weird but I can't remember the name of that school. We played the game on a cold late fall day. I wonder if it may have been in the first week of December it was so cold. The ground was still soft but you didn't want to fall down because your little tee shirt would be wet and stay wet. The game was tight. I don't remember the score but we won by a goal and then all hell broke lose. A couple of guys who had slid down and gotten all muddy and cold in the game slid down into a few big puddles. They didn't care that they were freezing because they couldn't feel anything because they were so happy. Some other guys joined in. The muddy guys started throwing mud on other guys and they got pissed off but then didn't care. Then even more guys slid into the mud puddles. They looked like they were having fun. Then it hit me, soccer was over, we won, no more torture, and so I got up some good speed and slide into a huge puddle and stood up covered in cold mud. Everybody was going nuts and yelling and throwing mud and more guys threw themselves into the freezing cold mud puddles, which were 6 feet long and 6 feet wide. The coaches were laughing their asses off but eventually yelled, "enough" and we climbed on the bus.

Everybody was muddy and guys started throwing mud. Now there was mud on the windows and some mud on the roof. Mud was all over the seats. This was thick dense mud that hung in place. We screamed and hollered the whole way home. When we got to the school the parents and clean, shinning, beautiful cheerleaders who had been at the game were there and some other cheerleaders as well. They were all screaming like we had conquered the world. The coach told us that the bus driver had something to say. The bus driver stood up and yelled at us like he was a wild man. He was furious. He was extremely pissed off and very angry. No one had even thought of the bus driver. We figured that he knew and understood what we had been through but he really had no idea. I could see that he was fuming and he told us that he was going to have to clean this bus and that it was going to be very difficult to clean. He told us that we were the worst bunch of kids he had ever met and that we should ashamed of ourselves. Then he sat down. Meanwhile the cheerleaders and parents are screaming their brains out like we were the Beatles or something. The coaches let us off the bus but I knew I had to say something to the bus driver. Looking back on it now I can see that I was always wise beyond my years.

I told the bus driver the two-year ordeal that we had been through. I told him about team try-outs and how hard it was to get on the team. I told him about kids that walked away from practice because they quit because the workouts everyday at practice were so painful. I told him about how the coaches, and I pointed right at the coaches, had tortured us "for our own good" and how at the end of practices they made us sprint up and down the length of the field until people were very close to passing out or puking. I told him about practices in late November when it was 45 degrees Fahrenheit and all we could wear were little shorts and tee shirts and that we would get windburn on our thighs and faces that would take a week to heal. I told him how we lost to that very team last year at that field but now we had won and how soccer was over and that we would never play another game with that same bunch of guys. I also told him that what he saw in this bus wasn't a big ugly mess but and explosion of unparalled joy. Joy, Joy, Joy. I told him that we are all so happy we slide into freezing cold puddles because it was the right thing to do. The look on his face got more and more relaxed as I told him all this. He looked over his shoulder at the mud and saw in a different light was he was looking at. I told him I was very sorry for the mess. I suggested that he get a hose and just hose the whole thing down. He thanked me and said something to the effect that maybe we weren't the worst bunch of kids he had ever seen. I turned to go out of the bus and my two coaches were looking at me like they had seen a ghost or something. They couldn't believe how eloquently I had expressed myself.

As I got inside and made my way into the locker room I heard a lot of girls screaming. I wondered what the hell is going on? I walked in the door and heard the screaming more clearly and I was horrified as to what I might see. The energy in the locker room was like nothing I had ever felt before. I was worried. I saw guys milling around the showers and some cheerleaders were holding open the other locker room door. And then one of our big guys came walking out of the shower still in his muddy cloths and he is soaked and he has a soaking wet cheerleader draped over his shoulder. There are not words to describe the look on my face. HOLY SHIT isn't going to cover it. The cheerleaders had lost their minds. I'd never seen anything like it. One or two other cheerleaders were dragged or carried into the showers until one of the coaches came in and he went BALLISTIC and the girls scattered. They got some parents to come into the gym and drag all the girls away. As fast as it had started it was over. I'm pretty sure it was big Dale Alhert who was big enough to carry a cheerleader on his shoulder. I'll tell you what; those two years of torture at the hands of our coaches was worth the 5 minutes of total calamity in our boy's locker room in the 9th grade. The cheerleaders were very happy for us. They no doubt felt like they were part of it because they were at a lot of our games. They also saw us walking up to the building after practices and they could see how badly we were beaten down at practices and so they probably felt a great deal of joy that all that pain and suffering was rewarded with a win. I'm telling you man…those girls went bonkers.

Let's get back to the musical discussion and my obsession with drumming. Boy, that was a fast transition. When 8th grade rolled around one of my best friends, Johnny, gave me a call to tell me his older brother Billy had bought a drum set. Before Johnny said another word I had slammed down the phone and flew out the door at top speed. I was always a very fast runner, very fast. I flew down the three flights of stairs in our apartment building and flew the little more than a quarter mile to Johnny's house I hurled myself into the kitchen via the little back door and scared the living crap out of Johnny's mom. Johnny stared at me in total disbelief. He was still standing next to the phone. I kid you not. They both stood startled and speechless and I said, 'Where are the drums, like a crazed maniac?" Johnny said, "There in the garage, the finished part of the garage. We went back there and when I saw the drums a wave of joy rushed over me. It was like a wave of energy that went from the drums past me. Even though they were not my drums I knew I was going to be playing them because nothing was going to stop me.

I proceeded to play those drums whenever I could. They were Billy's drums so I had to ask permission. That was so painful for me. He often wasn't around. He must have been six or seven years older than us. Billy was probably working somewhere. You may be wondering what does all this drumming stuff have to do with. "The Third Floor Movie Mystery?" Well, I am establishing the back-story of how much I'd love drumming and how it was a lifelong dream to get into a great band. The phrase "Third Floor" was a very important part of the name of the great band I eventually became a part of.

This went on for months where I had to ask Billy for permission to play. Eventually I couldn't take it anymore and I would play anyway. He caught me several times and he would yell and yell. Billy was not a tall guy but man oh man did he have muscles. He could toss me around like a rag doll. I was a skinny little guy but I was tough as nails. He never hit me but he did scare the crap out of me. Man, I can feel it like it is yesterday. I had a proposition for him. I said that I would keep the drums really clean and in tune. I would also use my paper route money to fix the broken things like the bass pedal and high hat. I told him I would make other upgrades like a new snare head when I got the money. To my amazement he said okay. So I took care of the drums and I could play whenever I wanted. I'm telling you right now that I played every day, after I delivered my papers and almost all day Saturday and Sunday. If Oprah existed at the time, she would have diagnosed me as obsessive- compulsive. I was a "crazy person" for drumming.

Eventually Billy played the drums less and less. He only knew how to play about 20 songs. He would play those songs again and again. He played much louder than me because he was so strong. I was working on learning every new song that came on the radio as well as, the Beatles, the Stones, David Bowie, the Dooby Brothers, Chicago. I also played to some Motown records that were there on the shelf. I loved Motown. Who didn't love Motown? One day I discovered that Billy was sometimes outside listening to me and he didn't know that I knew he was there. I knew this one night because I could see the exhale of his breath on a cold night. There was a light on the outside of the door and it illuminated the window so you could see outside. He was spying on me a little bit and listening in. That's just the normal human curiosity.

I was obsessed with drumming and I got better and better. One day I propositioned Billy with the idea that I would buy out the drums from him. I wanted to own these drums so bad. We agreed on a price of $40 or so, from what I remember. The deal was I could pay him no less than five dollar payments. I had a paper route and an allowance from my Mom and I was always mature for my age and I paid off Billy in a somewhat timely fashion. You had to be 13 to have a paper route so I know I was 13 when this was all going down. I eventually paid him off and the drums were mine! No one could sell them away from under me and no one could tell me when I could or couldn't play. I was so happy in that stage in my life I can't even explain it. I felt like a joy, fulfilled, multimillionaire. I had named that great place to hang out and drum in as the Rock Room. I remember when I graduated from 9'th grade I went to Johnny's house, out to the finished, carpeted, heated, comfy part of the garage and played Alice Cooper's, "School's Out" about four or five times in a row with note for note perfection. I played each take, a little heavy in order to express my bursting joy as a result of being freed from Jr. High school.

How can I talk about drumming and not mention Buddy Rich? Buddy Rich was a god among men. He was super natural. The way he played the drums was not to be fathomed. He did things that left you as a drummer, in shock and disbelief. He may decide to do some long work on the snare that no other human on Earth could reproduce. When I mean long work I mean 4 or 5 minutes. His chops were beyond smooth. I think I can summarize his playing in this way. Buddy Rich played the drums as if God the eternal creator of all that is took physical form and played the drums. I think that sums it up pretty well. You yourself could practice the things you saw Buddy Rich do but, you would never come close to doing exactly what he did in 1,000 years. I used to see Buddy on the TV during afternoon talk shows that were big in their day. He used to show up on the Merv Griffin Show and the Mike Douglas show. They were both day- time talk shows that were like The Tonight show with Johnny Carson. Not a lot of people know this but Johnny Carson played the drums.

I would see Buddy on one of those shows and I would see some mind blowing thing he did on the snare and I would try like hell for weeks to try to reproduce it with some proficiency. By constantly trying to play like Buddy I developed some mean chops. I fell far short of Buddy's chops but my 1/3 level Buddy chops were pretty smoking hot. When it came to playing some 4 beat song on the radio it was like a walk in the park. The biggest thing for me as a drummer eventually got to the point of just remembering all of the songs I knew how to play. It got more and more difficult to remember all the nuances and drum fills throughout the songs. That is where having that tape recorder in my brain came in handy. While I was sitting in history class or something in Jr. High School and while other kids were paying attention, maybe, I was playing the Chicago song, "Does Anybody Know What Time It Is," over and over again in my brain. After decades of this I'm telling you I have some kind of super computer drumming brain. I can assure you that most really good musicians are super freaks.

By half way through that summer, after 9th grade, with me getting bigger and stronger than ever. I beat those drums to death. They just started to fall apart. The cymbals were warped and flat sounding. Several of the toning pins on the drumheads were just stripped. That's really bad. You can't tune the drum properly. The base drum foot pedal had almost no spring action left in it and so I took those drums to their death.

You'll love this. We did a "WHO" job on that room. I had told Johnny what I wanted to do. I wanted to invite over my friends and his friends. We had to smuggle some beer from his dad. We had to try to find a little bit of pot. We didn't get either. We had to settle for cigarettes, which was a big score. We also had soda. We had a good mix of girls and boys. The totally smoking hot Jenna Soldak was there. She was a gymnast and she was so hot. Lord save us all. I put on a good 45 minutes or so of drumming while playing along to music and on the last song I started to kick my drums over like "THE WHO" did. I told everybody to go nuts and to just break things. They were timid at first. They threw a few pillows and some empty soda bottles around. I said, "No, trash the place." I told them, "I am done here!" I told them that we can break this place up. I started to flip chairs and to smash week drum shells with my feet. People caught on. Someone ripped a couch cushion and all this white fluffy stuff came flying out. I had been putting up with this complete piece of crap stereo and I picked it up and slammed it on the ground. People couldn't believe it when I did that, then everybody, even the girls, went mental. It was like a food fight with the drums and beat up home furnishings. When everything was broken into pieces and everybody flopped down on the floor from exertion it was so fantastic. The feathers were still flying in the air and someone started laughing, and then someone else started and then we were all laughing ourselves into hysterics. It was like we still had pent up energy to release from having graduated from junior high. I provided everybody with an opportunity to go nuts and man did they ever. I'll never forget that day as long as I live. You can't believe the amount of tension and stress that exists just below the surface, even in pretty, quiet girls. We smashed everything to pieces. No one cared. It was all pretty much junky stuff to begin with and so I knew we weren't going to get in trouble.

CHAPTER FOUR

HIGH SCHOOL AND LED ZEPPELIN

During high school I was totally 100% focused on Ice Hockey. I still loved music and I listened to the radio and records constantly. I had a pretty good record collection and my older brothers Hughie, and Kenny both had record collections. There was always a lot of interesting music to listen to. Back in those days people loaned out albums to people all the time. Money was scarce and so it was great when a friend of yours loaned you a new album and you had something new to listen to for a couple of days. My brothers had albums like, Humble Pie (30 days in the hole), Black Sabbath, Jethro Tull, the Moody Blues, Yes- Fragile, Janis Joplin, Led Zeppelin, Jefferson Airplane, Procol Harum, David Bowie, Bob Dylan, the Beatles and all kinds of other groovy stuff. I should point out that my dad was still alive and he lived in Quakertown. He had bought for himself a high end organ and when he had a few beers in him he got into some heavy jams of his own. His upper body would sway back and forth ever so slowly as he drew out certain chords and phrases. He was playing the kind of stuff that you could see on the Lawrence Welk show. The Organ had a built in drum machine that could play drum beats like the waltz and the Bossa Nova and other jazzy south American influenced beats. Sometimes I would turn the organ on just to play the different drumbeats and I would try to tap along with my fingers. I'm so glad that my dad had such a nice organ to play in his final years of life. I was talking to my mom on the phone a few days ago and she told me that my dad took accordion lessons after the war when they lived down on Belmar Terrace in Philadelphia. My mom told me that my dad took lessons on the Accordion and he practiced a lot and that he stood in the same place in the room and that he had worn off the shellac on the floor where he tapped his foot to keep time. Now I know where I get my obsessive-compulsive hard work tendencies from. I was the last child born as mentioned earlier and I don't have any memories of my dad playing the Accordion.

Although my love of music was very intense I also still loved movies and when ever a new big movie came out my friends and I would get money from our parents to go to the theater. There was only one theater in Lansdale back in those days. Theaters in those days only had one or two movies in-house at a time. They had the matinee showing during the afternoon and they would play the G rated movie and in the evening they played a PG or R rated movie. I always loved going to the movies. Who didn't? I was amazed at cinemas ability to get under people's skin. You could be in a theater and one of the toughest guys around could be there with his parents and a brother or sister. The tough guy didn't know you were there. If you tilted your head back and looked back a few rows you could see his face. You could see something there in the theater that you would never see in school in 100 years and that is, Mr. tough guy looking like he's about to cry at the end of the movie. I learned in junior high school when "Old Yeller" came out that movies have the power to break your heart in two. Another movie that broke my heart in two was "Brian's Song." I cried and cried at the end of that movie just as I did for, "Old Yeller."

So while in high school I was tremendously focused on Ice Hockey. I didn't have a drum set at my disposal. It bothered me but I knew I wasn't going to put a band together in high school. What would be the point in that? We're all too young to drink and to get into the bars and clubs. I focused on Ice Hockey with the idea in the back of my mind that I might go pro. I had played street hockey like a mad man for about four years. I even played in the league that was held at Whites Road Park. Whites Road Park had a big swimming pool in the summer and the ice-skating rink in the winter. The "boards" at the rink were made of two layers of three-quarter inch plywood that was bolted into iron pipes that were about 3 inches across. There was no give in these "boards" at all! We ran at full speed during whole games under a sweltering summer sun with sweat pouring down our faces. Guys who were six-inches taller and weighed 40 pounds more than my friends and I would slam us at almost full speed into these, "boards." Some times the pain was disturbing. You knew you were just really hurt but you kept your feet moving while chasing after that stupid little orange ball. Other times you would double over onto the ground and you would see flashes of light. Even though there was a referee he just happened to not notice a thing. No one can ever question my toughness or the toughness of every kid who played in that league.

Some kids who weren't "crazy tough" like us just walked away during games. They had more sense. I figure the situation was they didn't have a "sick in the head" older brother who beat them up all of their lives for no reason. Kids who had crazy older brothers were used to the pain and psychological abuse. This league had an 18-year and older division. Fights broke out in those games all the time. The cops had to be called to regain order. The ambulance had to be called quite often. During the second season the police department sent an officer to watch the 18 and older games. The cop was there to watch the games live so he could see what was going on rather than to have to listen to all of the screaming viewpoints when they showed up after having been called on the radio. The fact that there was a cop car there and a cop caused more people to stand and watch the games. We can thank the Broad Street Bullies for all of this carryover energy of insanity and toughness. So now with a police officer there to watch the action the young men out there still carried on like barbarians. Some kids were there to play hockey and some guys were there to do one thing; hurt people. I dealt with guys like that when I played street hockey and ice hockey. Well, even with a cop there all hell broke loose again and again. They would have to call the ambulance again and again. Sometimes the cop would have to call for backup. At some point in the second season of the White Road's park street hockey league, it was shut down. It was costing too much police time and too many serious injuries occurred. If you plan on going to war, recruit your young men from Lansdale Pennsylvania.

It was so fantastic when years later I was back at that location but now I was playing Ice Hockey. We were using that rink the proper way. We were using that rink for the sport it was designed for. Some of my earliest memories are from that rink. I played in my first game against a real opponent there when we had a scrimmage against a different school. My mother and sister both came out to see me play and it was a brutally freezing cold winter day and they stood there freezing in order to watch me play. It is a fantastic memory. What a joy to be playing in that rink flying around on the proper surface, which is ice, and to be able to play the game as it was designed. It was a real feeling of maturity for me as a young athlete. Several years later, after I was out of high school someone told me they tore the boards down. I couldn't believe what they were telling me. They said that the ice rink was no longer viable and so there were no need to have the boards there and so they tore them down. The cement floor of the rink is still there but it's used for parking now. What a total drag. There is a real special feeling about being outside on a cold day or cold night while playing Ice Hockey. Your cheeks get all rosy red and your nose runs and your eyes get dried out and you have to blink a lot to keep your eyes moist. The puck's thud into the boards sends a reverberating sound into the dark night. I was really sad when I heard that they were shutting down the Whites Road rink. I have very special memories from those days. We were a bunch of real serious hockey players. We were Knights. Our colors were light blue and dark blue. We were North Penn Ice Hockey!

I taught myself how to skate all through the 10th grade. Man oh man is it hard to learn how to skate on ice hockey skates that have no teeth in the front. I fell on my ass again and again and again. Let's talk about my dear mom and how many times she drove me, and a few teammates back and forth from practice. Now that I think about it I realize that my mom was a hockey mom! Oh My God. My mom was a hockey mom. She really was kind of like a taxi service that is on call constantly. I hope I thanked her enough in those days. I tried out for the team in the summer before 11th grade, that's right in the summer and I made the team. A lot of guys did not make the team and I felt so bad for those guys. A few months later I was named as the captain of the team. I was stunned that the coach picked me to be the captain of the team. It wasn't until we played many games that I realized the responsibilities that went along with being the captain. I already knew the rules of the game well and that was very important because I was able to argue with the referee effectively. On many occasions I caught the referee making mistakes. We went from losing games 13-0, 12-1, 10-1, to eventually losing by scores like 4-1, 4-2, 3-1. My buddy Stan and I lifted weights at the local YMCA 3 to 4 times a week. Even though I only weighed 135 pounds when I played hockey I was strong as hell. If I decided I was going to deck you, you can rest assured that you were going to be lying on your back on the ice. I played left-wing and my buddy Stan anchored the defense. We snuck into the playoffs and did the unthinkable. First we beat Council Rock who had a very good team. They had a great big guy on defense that you wanted to avoid at all cost. Then we did that which is truly astonishing. We beat the mighty Tenet. You just can't imagine what that means. They used to destroy us in the regular season. It wasn't even close. They would toy with us the way a cat toys with a tired and captured mouse. When we won that championship game my teammates and I went ballistic. It is not like any feeling you could never describe. We were Kings of all we surveyed, Kings of the world. You shift into an other worldly feeling. Your whole body weighs less than a feather. We all swarmed towards our goalie and threw our gloves and sticks into the air. We all hugged and high fived each other over and over again. Shear joy was shooting out of everyone's eyes. Our coach, Tony Cooperburg is a God amongst men and our assistant coach Shane Galdo was an excellent teacher. They both helped the team get better so that we were more effective at winning in tight situations. We rode our school bus with each side of the bus full of my teammates with our hands out of the windows showing the number one finger while screaming, "We are number one, yeah" all the way down Main Street in Lansdale. I told these guys how it was done because I had done it three times before in Jr. High School. We woke people up out of their drab winter blues as they walked along Main St. at night. People were honking their horns and waving back at us. It was a friggin blast I tell ya.

When I was a senior I was a much better player. I scored a lot more goals and had many assists. I was the best guy on offense and my old best friend Stan, who was a junior, was the best guy on defense. Stan was a big strong guy and he was a hell of a hockey player. You would not want to cross Stan's path if he was in a foul mood. We had a really good goalie, Rolly, and a tough bunch of sound hockey players. I got my driver's license on the day I tuned 16 and I had a Chevy Biscayne, which is a huge vehicle. I drove 4 guys and myself to endless practices and we listened to almost nothing but Led Zeppelin. The car was huge and the trunk could hold loads of hockey equipment. Believe it or not we got high a bunch of times while driving to practice. It was a very different time back in those days. Our assistant coach drove a Falcon and when we drove to practice we were just Falcon around! In my senior year we were unfortunately eliminated the first round of the playoffs. I don't want to name the school that defeated us because I am still pissed off about the whole situation 30 years later.

Although I didn't have drums at my disposal I always had sticks and I would drum away on the edge of the mattress. I would sometimes set up my schoolbooks and note pads on the bed to get different tones and would play along to records like that. I was also always tapping my fingers in class. Just like grade school and junior high school I got in trouble all the time in high school for tapping my fingers constantly. People knew of me in high school as a good drummer based solely on the stories of my accomplishments in junior high. I really enjoyed this fact and I acted like a drummer guy because I knew in my heart of hearts that I was going to be a drummer in a band and I was going to lay down the beat so people could dance and forget their worries.

During high school I listened to Led Zeppelin constantly. I could write a book about my love of Led Zeppelin. I loved the album Physical Graffiti. Only God knows how many times I listened to that album on cassette on my portable boombox. I was also a huge fan of RUSH. I listened to both RUSH and Led Zeppelin all during my junior high years and High School years. It is safe to say that RUSH and Led Zeppelin were my two favorite bands. Since I was a drummer I really looked up to Neil Peart and John Bonham. I analyzed their every move. Even though I didn't have drums to play I was working out the drum tracks in my mind so I knew what to do in the future when I did eventually get drums again. Between myself, and my two brothers we had all of the Led Zeppelin albums. I had a few albums on cassette so I could listen to them on my boom box when I was outside. There were three cassette tapes that I listened to so many times that I broke them. The first one was "Physical Graffiti" by Led Zeppelin. The second one was by Earth Wind and Fire and that album was called "That's the Way of the World." The third was by Lynyrd Skynyrd and it was called "Gold and Platinum Band." All of my friends were obsessed with Zeppelin as well. The mighty Zep was everywhere. Led Zeppelin owned the 1970's. When I got older, in my mid twenties, I could play Zeppelin extremely well. Friends of mine would just sit there and watch me play along to the music. I became a part of the music. It was so incredible. Playing the drums to "When the Levee Breaks" is hypnotic.

When I used to visit my dad at Melody Lakes in Quakertown there was a Sears surplus store. It was a small store. There was a blue sparkle, again with the blue sparkle, drum set in the window. It looked out of place. There were no other drum sets or other musical equipment there. It was very strange. My dad and I would sometime shop over near that Sears store and he could see me eyeing up the drums. I used to talk to my mom all the time about getting drums. She always said no, very firmly. After all we lived in an apartment complex. My older brothers also always heard me talking about wishing I could have a set of drums. That's all I ever did was talk about one day having a set of drums to play. I told my dad about wishing I had drums as well. Well guess what sports fans, have I got a story for you. Like I had told you my dad lived at Melody Lakes in Quakertown. It was a trailer park and retirement type community. There were and still are some really nice trailer homes there. I have always liked going out in the woods and wandering around. There were woods right next to my Dad's home. There would be a fair amount of those little white floaty things flying around in the air. You know what I mean; those little white fluffy feathery things that you grab and make a wish upon. Well I got more and more desperate about owning a set of drums even though I really didn't have a place to play. Even if I didn't have a place to play at least I would feel so much more complete with the knowledge that I had drums. I kept wishing on those a little magical white floaty things. I would grab one out of the air as they floated by, and I would close my eyes and make a wish.

A few months go by and I am up at my father's place. I remember distinctly wishing one more time for some drums before we went over to my brother Pat's mobile home for a visit. My brother Kenny who was living with Pat at the time was there as well. My mom and my brother Hughie were driving up from Lansdale. At one point while I'm eating a piece of fancy chocolate someone says, "Hey Dan we have a surprise for you." I'm just now remembering that it was my birthday because there are pictures of me opening presents. They walked me over to what was Kenny's bedroom door. Someone opens the door and there is a beautiful new blue sparkle drum set! I went into a state of shock because I dropped the piece of chocolate I was eating and had no memory of that. My dad and my older brothers had chipped in and bought the drums for me. How do you like them apples? I sat down on the drums and was able to hold a beat but I was really rusty. That was one of the happiest days of my life. My brother Hughie got out his acoustic guitar and we played together for about 60 minutes.

So guess what happened next? I had no where to play the drums and I had to pack them away in my storage locker in the apartment complex laundry room next to where I kept my hockey equipment. They sat there unused but at least I had them for when circumstances changed. The following December, which was just four months after I was given the drums my dad died. He was 60. All of those years of smoking and drinking caught up with him. He had a really bad hip. He had bone on bone, which is extremely painful. He never did exercise as a result of the bad hip. His unhealthy lifestyle led to his early demise but that was how Dad's lived back in those days. I was only 16. I was a junior in high school. I was one of those kids who when he graduated from high school he was only 17. I turned 18 three months after graduation. One of the last things he did for me was to buy me those drums. Drums that were going to get a ton of use a few years later when my best friend moved into an apartment down in Germantown, Pennsylvania which he lived in during his college years.

My dad, the musician, buys a dream for his son, the musician.

CHAPTER FIVE
THE COLLEGE YEARS

I was so happy to be out of high school. There was no way I was going on to more schooling. No way. I thought all of the people who were signing up for more schooling were flat out crazy. I had no intention of going to college, until I found out that most of my friends from the local neighborhood were going to college. I was so focused on Ice Hockey and my Ice Hockey friends that I had drifted away from some of my best friends in my neighborhood. There was one guy who I didn't think was very smart at all and he was going to college. The last I had talked to him he had said that he was going to focus on being a carpenter. There was a time when I was in junior high school that I too thought about being a carpenter. It got me to thinking that maybe I was screwing something up here.

None of my brothers or sister had graduated from college. My older brother of four years, Hughie, was going to Montgomery County Community College, also known by the locals as Montco. I couldn't believe my eyes as I watched my brother go from a Mr. tough guy personality into a total nerd type personality. It got to the point where he would study hour after hour day after day. There were times that my mother and I would yell at him to go outside. Go get some fresh air in your lungs boy. It seemed so strange that he would talk so much about how he loved classes and his professors. I know he hated high school, like I did, and yet there he was, totally loving college. I was perplexed to say the least.

31

I decided I had to go because pretty much everybody I knew, except one best friend, was going so I better get on the ball before I am left out and I didn't want to be left out. While going to the local community college, Montco, I played in my second year of Men's league Ice Hockey. I played my first year of Men's league Ice Hockey when I was just a senior in high school. I only weighed 135 pounds but I could skate like the wind. We were the Trevose Wings and my buddy Stan and I joined the team because our coach Tony Cooperburg played on the team. He told us that teammates of his just saw us practicing, at Whites Road rink, and they wanted us to join the team. It was a total honor. We played the Bucks County Bucks and beat them in an un-believably violent 3 game finals. The level of violence was off the charts. We had a lot of really good players on our team. My coach Tony Cooperburg was there as well was our assistant coach Shane Galdo. Shane was a hell of a hockey player too. He always had a full beard, which made him look so menacing to Stan and I because we were young high school kids. I considered it to be an honor to be on the same team as Shane Galdo. Tony's younger brother who I hope I am remembering this right was named John. He was even stronger than Tony, which is hard to imagine. If I tried to check Tony all I heard was a metal sound like I was bumping into a fire hydrant. If you try to check Johnny you heard a similar sound but it was a denser metal. I can't remember the names of the other players but they were all very skilled. Our goalie's name was Bock and he was a solid goalie.

There was one time when two guys stood at center ice and started smashing each other with their sticks. It was like hand to hand combat. Both of them broke their sticks over the other guy's body and then they started sword fighting with their broken sticks. Those two guys had gone insane. I kid you not, this really happened. Everybody on both benches started screaming at the tops of their lungs to get the referees attention so that he could skate over there to the warring players. All he could do is get as close as possible to the players and blow his brains out into his whistle hoping the shrill sound would bring the players back to reality. This would cause all of the guys on the ice to follow the ref and they could start to separate their own player away from the madness. I am not making this story up. The violence out there was really disturbing and I cannot believe that I was 17 and I was out there playing in the middle of a war on ice. I weighed 135 pounds for crying out loud.

After we finally won the championship game some of us went out on the ice with a large silver bowl that we were awarded and we drank champagne out of it. We were all in stages of undress. Some guys had their jerseys off as well as their shoulder and elbow pads. We skated around sipping champagne from this very large bowl and as far as I am concerned I won the Stanley Cup. You should have seen the welts and bruises and open cuts on all of our bodies. Our captain's name was Donee. He was of Irish decent and was crazy and full of life. I'll never forget Donee as long as I live. Some of the players from the Bucks team came out of their locker and glared at us. They wanted to kill us. You could feel their anger upon you. But we were the victors and we earned our victory lap.

We played the Bucks County Bucks again the following year in the Championship finals. I was in my first year at Montco. Our Trevose Wings team was pretty much intact as it was also for the Bucks County Bucks. Let me tell you something; it was all out war from the drop of the first puck of the first game. Every single shift mattered like your life was on the line. If you made one tiny mistake a guy on the other team would capitalize on it. We had been playing each other throughout the regular season and every one of those games was out of control. Now that it was the finals the level of intensity and insanity was ratcheted up a notch. Let me tell you this. The Bucks County Bucks were not going to be denied. They were not going to allow us to win that trophy two years in a row. As strong as a team as we were they still were not going to allow us to win. They eventually won the third game, beating us two games to one. I didn't play in that league any more because I valued my health. It took three months, even as a young man, for my body to truly heal after one of those seasons down at The Face-Off rink in Warminster, Pennsylvania.

I took a year off of playing Ice Hockey in the wintertime. I did play two more seasons as a "Penquin" with my best friend Stan at the General Washington Rink in Audubon, PA. We were the Penquins in tribute to the fact that we knew Ray Talfield who made it to the pros and played for the Pittsburgh Penquins when they won two Stanley Cup championships. I used to skate and hang out with Ray at the White's Road rink. Ray went to North Penn High School and he was one year ahead of me. The White's Road rink is gone as is the Melody Brook rink in Chalfont, which was the rink where I played my first year of pick-up hockey games during Open Hockey sessions. Peggy Fleming once skated there in her preparations for the Olympics. The two brothers who ran the rink had a picture of Miss Fleming on the wall and it brought both men much joy. The George Washington Rink is gone as well now. The Face-Off rink where 90% of my Ice Hockey action took place is still there but they changed the name and they added a new rink to the location. Local Ice Hockey still thrives. The Winter Sport Skating Rink is still there which is really amazing. I don't know how old that rink is but it is very old. The people who run that facility should be very proud of their dedication to that rink.

I finally quit playing Ice Hockey, much to my buddy Stan's dismay. Stan's older Don actually eventually even got involved with playing Ice Hockey. Stan and I had been through hell together. Stan was always bigger than me so his body could handle the punishment easier than mine. I finally had a growth spurt after high school and suddenly I weighed 165 pounds and grew an inch or so. I ran into some old friends and they couldn't believe how much bigger I was. It was really strange. If I could have played all of my high school Ice Hockey time at 165 pounds and then had a growth spurt that took me up to 195 pounds then maybe my dream of being a professional Ice Hockey player would have been more realistic. My body and mind could no longer deal with the uncontrolled violence of Ice Hockey. My old buddy Stan went on to play for RIT or the Rochester Institute of Technology.

As soon as I knew I was done with hockey I became 100% focused on becoming a world famous drummer. Have you heard of me?

My best friend Phil and I became inseparable. We formed a very tight musical alliance. This alliance stayed intact for many, many years. In fact it was fourteen years.

I first met Phil in Junior high school. We were on the soccer team together. I hung out over at his house a lot. His family was very nice. All of his older brothers were star athletes. His younger brothers also ended up being star athletes in their individual endeavors. Phil and I sat next to each other for a whole year of science class in the ninth grade. In the 10th grade during Biology class he sat in front and to the left of me. Phil switched in high school from playing soccer to wrestling. Even though in reality we didn't spend that much time with each other in high school there was still a tight friendship there. You have to understand that there were 700 people in our class, and so there were

2100 students in our school. It is a very easy to drift from one another when there is that many people around. Phil saw me drum a lot back in the Rock Room in junior high school. He always thought of me as a rock-n-roll drummer dude.

The way my musical career started was when one of my old friends was having of high school reunion party at his parent's house in the late summer of 1982. We had graduated in May of 1980. I said to someone standing there that I am so bored with life. I told him that I am officially starting a band right now. I said this to a guy who had been in my homeroom all through high school and he says to me, "Yeah, I play bass." I couldn't believe it. I said to him, "Are you serious?" And he says, "yes." It was so unbelievably strange. Then he says to me, "I have a cousin who is an incredible guitar player. He is the best guitarist in all of North Penn high school." I said to him something like, "You've got to be kidding me?" He says "no." I was flabbergasted as to how fast it happened. I was literally just thinking out loud and just like that, standing on Tizzy's lawn I had the makings of a band. My buddy Phil was standing right there so I got his attention and I said, "You're going to be a singer in my band and don't give me any crap." He said, "What are you kidding me?" I said, "No I'm not kidding you. There is something that you don't know about yourself and that is that you have a strong voice and it projects very well. You could be a good singer." He just kind of laughed at me. Believe it or not folks that's how fast it happened. This guy's name was Rick Mosley and we made arrangements to get together. Phil did end up being the singer.

A few days later I got together with Rick at his place and I met his wife Faye. Yeah that's right they were married already just two years out of high school. I knew Faye fairly well because she was also in my homeroom all through high school. Faye was pretty good-looking and she was more of a quiet person. It just so happens that she also played the keyboards. She wasn't that good in the beginning but she got better and better. I dug out my blue sparkle drums that my dad and brothers had bought for me three years prior and now they were finally going to get some use. Phil had a roommate whose name was Jack. Those guys were sharing an apartment down in Germantown because they were going to college at the Philadelphia College of Textiles and Sciences. It's not called that name anymore. Phil brought Jack along and Jack would listen to us from the very beginning of our sessions and you could tell he wanted to play. We eventually met the soon to be legendary guitar player Brit Kole. Man oh man could he play. I'm not sure if he was a Junior or a senior in high school but it didn't really matter with how well he could play. He played a Gibson SG circa 1974 and it was a deep red wine color. He was only 16 and was in the 10th grade! By the time the band broke up he was 17. We all started playing on a regular schedule in August 1982 at Rick and Faye's house on Broad Street in Lansdale near the railroad tracks. It takes months for a band to gel. We all stuck with it because all of us got enjoyment out of it. Rick and Faye had jobs, Brit was in high school, and Jack, Phil and I were all going to college full time. By the time we all got together on the weekends we were ready to rock. Our new friend Jack made wicked, Kamikazes and so we were all drinking beer and doing the occasional Kamikaze. Jack did buy a guitar, and he quickly signed up to take lessons and got better and better. Before you knew it he was playing rhythm guitar at first with his amplifier turned down and then as he got better he was told to turn the hell up. We were called, "On The Rock's." We argued for days as to what our band name was going to be. Trying to get six people to agree on anything is difficult but trying to get six musicians to agree on a band name is really difficult. We played just cover tunes. We played some really good Cream songs like "Tales of Brave Ulysses" and "Sunshine of your Love", and some Led Zeppelin songs such as, "Communication Breakdown" and "The Rover." Some of the other songs we played were, Born to be Wild, Lonely is the Night, The Seeker, and our masterpiece, "Gloria." Brit was the star of the band as he could really wail. The dust wore off of my stiffness and pretty soon my old chops were coming back in a big way. We all got stronger together. We played really loud and we had a blast. When I would walk up the steps to go take a leak in the bathroom I would have the biggest smile on my face because I was realizing a dream and this band seemed to pop up out of nowhere. We had a nice living room to jam in, a whole bunch of good equipment and a refrigerator bursting with cold beer. What more could a happy young drummer ask for. After we had gotten pretty good we would usually have a few people hanging around the house either in the living room, kitchen or sometimes out on the porch if it wasn't too cold. Two of the main dudes who hung out were Phil's youngest brother Blaine and Brit's younger brother Gary. Those two guys became good friends and remained friends for over a decade.

I have to take a second to share a quick thought out of nowhere. I do apologize.

One thing that I can tell you that absolutely cracked me up, was when I first saw the character "Animal" the drummer from Sesame Street. For years on end whenever they showed him in brief little blurbs I would laugh histerically. The reason I laughed so hard is because I often felt the way he "looked." He was always flailing away while acting half insane and that is actually how real drumming often feels. You have to have yourself on a razor's edge of madness while maintaining intense blistering concentration. Some songs are worse than others for sure. Many RUSH songs are a painful blur. God almighty, how I love that wild red haired maniac.

For a minute there I thought that we never did any outside gigs but in fact we did do one good gig outside of the house. We played outdoors at the Philadelphia College of Textiles and Sciences. The college was having some sort of outdoor celebration day in the spring and Phil lined us up there to play live outside. Phil was head DJ of the college radio station. There were a lot of people there. People were throwing Frisbees and kicking soccer balls around. There was a long stone wall and it was full of people sitting with their feet hanging over the side. At one point while I was drumming to a song that has a driving four beat, Phil got my attention and pointed to the people sitting on the stonewall and every single person was swinging their legs to the beat. I got a real big smile on my face seeing that. It is weird but it made me happy to see people unconsciously rocking along to the beat.

We broke up in June 1983, for the most part, because Rick and Faye were sick and tired of having a rock band's crap taking up their whole living room. It just happened one afternoon where Rick pretty much started yelling and Faye joined in and it was obvious no matter what anyone else said that the band was through. It was really hard to take but we all knew it couldn't last forever. We had to carry out all of our stuff right then and there. You should have seen all of the amps, drums, guitars and wires. There are always wires everywhere. "This confusion, wires."

Brit Kole did go on to become a Sony Music recording artist with the band called Echolyn. When he got out of high school he formed a local band called Narcissus with a bunch of really talented musicians. Brit is a really talented guitar player. He could also sing. He went on to study recording engineering so that he could have the knowledge to be involved in that aspect of music production as well.

When "On The Rock's" broke up Phil, Jack, and I naturally formed a band together. Since those guys lived together as college roommates and were good friends it was a natural and easy thing to do. When I was in Lansdale I was either working, at class, or doing my homework but all of the rest of the time I was down there in Germantown constantly. We called ourselves, "SNAFU." We chose this band name because Phil had found the word in the dictionary. I didn't think a word like that existed. Do you know what it stands for? It stands for Situation Normal All Fucked Up! Do you believe that? Is that not fantastic? Phil showed me the word in the dictionary because I didn't believe him. It's an old military word that they used in World War II jargon. Jack didn't have an objection to it and so we became "SNAFU."

I had given Phil one of my brother Hughie's old classical guitars and Phil started practicing. Jack and Phil played guitars constantly. Phil took to song writing quicker then Jack did. Phil also bought a little Casio keyboard and he messed around with that a lot. Sometimes that damn Casio kept him up all night. We did something pretty surprising because we decided to focus on writing our own original music. Phil and Jack eventually were so good at guitar that if we decided to play a cover song those guys could figure out the guitar work. Since I had been such a heavy drummer in junior high school I was further along than those guys were in their musicianship. All of our early songs were pretty simple because those guys were pretty much beginners as musicians. They had both obviously rocked their brains out in, "On The Rocks" but now Brit was not there to carry the tune. Plus when you're writing new songs for the first time you don't create masterpieces. Each song that Phil wrote, got better and better and Jack and I helped polish them to completion. After about two years when Phil was going to write a song he could pretty much visualize what he was thinking and was able to put it together more quickly. We did a lot of real recording in the radio station, which was way, way up the stairs in this big old building on campus. It was the student center building and we got to climb several different stairwells to get up to our cool little studio in the sky. We used to get high up there all the time. It was just the coolest place to hang out and record. It was a tiny room. It was no bigger than 10' x 12'. There was a Reel- to- Reel machine there that Phil learned how to operate. We were able to do overdubs and backing vocals. It was really, really cool. As stated earlier Phil was the top DJ so we owned that space. When various students wandered up because they saw the light in the sky we would let them into the room and they thought that it was awesome that we were jamming and recording up there. No one ever bothered us or gave us a hard time. We recorded about a dozen songs that met our intense standards. Some of the titles are, "This First One", "Why Don't You Realize", "Pretense", "Fleeting Melody", "Not Trying to Fight You", and "Little Boy." Those two guys wrote a song together and didn't want my input on it and it was called "War."

About a year after those guys graduated from "Textile" in 1984, Phil and I started to drift from Jack. Jack lived in New Jersey after he lived for a short while in Bloomsburg, Pennsylvania. I think you could say that SNAFU died in the fall of 1985. We had a SNAFU reunion once in Phil's parent's house down in the basement in the Rock Room II on November 11th. We recorded the session on the four-track machine that Phil had bought and the session was super powerful. We recorded a bunch of songs from the old days but we also recorded two of Jack's songs. They were called "Smile Again" and "Triumph." Smile Again is a sad lilting song while Triumph has a catchy off-beat, beat to it. Jack should be extremely proud of himself for writing those songs. They were both catchy tunes. We have a rendition of "Glass Blower" that is legendary, as far as I'm concerned. Jack played guitar on this song while Phil focused 100% on singing his guts out. Jack had his amp turned way up and his guitar sounded ominous. *He had his amp turned up to 11.* The situation that WAS normal, got all Fucked Up!!!

CHAPTER SIX

POST COLLEGE: FREE TO ROAM

Now that Phil was home we set up shop in his parent's house. His dad put up a wall so we could have an enclosed space. His parents knew we were serious musicians. Him and I wrote all kinds of songs together. He wrote the music and the lyrics and I created another totally cool drum track. We each bought better equipment. In fact my good old Sears surplus blue sparkle kit was falling apart. They really were. Phil stepped up and did an amazing thing. He bought a brand-new drum set. He loved drumming like mad. I watched Phil drum like a wild man on his text books in college and he destroyed his books. He became obsessed like most drummers do. It was like a drug to him. Every day after work he would race home to play his drums. The brand name of the drums was Yamaha and they were black and shiny. The kit came with some new cymbals so we could get rid of some of the old flat sounding cymbals. He kept getting better and better as a drummer. On one evening I Knighted him as a drummer. I placed a drum stick from one shoulder to the other and declared him to be a member of "The Order of the Realm of Drummers." I was his teacher so he was learning from one of the best. He also bought a new electronic keyboard. The old Casio was a little thing that sounded really cheesy. The new keyboard had all sorts of far out sounds we could add to our songs. We wrote so many songs and they were good songs. We played them again and again and we heard and felt the songs get stronger and stronger. We did a lot of recording of songs on the 4-Track recorder he had bought. We played the songs over and over until we got an excellent base track and then we could do overdubs of vocals or percussion. We were intense perfectionist. We developed chops between ourselves that were so tight it was diabolical. Our powers of telepathy between us were mind-boggling. Quite often, when we were jamming, we would just rock out together and it was 100% improvisation. We had become as one! Guitar and drums as one! Some of the song titles from those days are, "Why the Bay", Mood de la Coca", I*You*We", "Wearing a Mask", "On Time – Off Time", "People" and "The Bridge Song." The song "On Time – Off Time" is a 12 minute experiment. I said to Phil, "Let's play a song for a long time and just let whatever happens happen. Don't stop if something gets weird, just keep going. Let's start the song by being complete idiots. Let's purposely mess the other guy up. Let's keep doing off time things. Don't let me settle into a beat. If you hear me doing a beat, mess it up. Then at some point well come back in together and rock our brains out." He said, "OK" and that's what we did. The beginning part which is about 5 minutes of goofy-ness turns into a song which is something I still listen do 29 years later. Keep in mind this is all 100% improvisation. We have no idea what is going to happen. We hit levels of Rock God stature that is hard to fathom. Phil plays the guitar at a level he never even came close to before. All of sudden he's coming up with stuff that had me hypnotized. When we were at the height of the song at about the ¾ mark he had a guitar sound like he was summoning forth the legions of Satan's army. Where did it come from?

After about two years of this phase of our Rock journey, luck struck. I found us a bass player. Remember when I told you that Brit Kole played in a good band called Narcissus? Well the bass player in that band was Scooter Ritnicks. He was a talented bass player. He really knew his stuff. I ran into him one night at school when I was going to Gwynedd Mercy College. I approached him and told him I knew he was a great bass player because I saw him at the Fifth Street Pub in Lansdale with Narcissus. Well that just made his day. He got a big ole smile on his face! We talked in the hallway between classes and hit it off immediately. In looking back on this stuff it is incredibly interesting to see how many things just magically fall into place.

Scott and I talked on the phone but to my surprise he wasn't ready to just jump into something. He said we had to have good vocals. He went on and on about how there are no good singers anywhere.

I said, "OK, OK. I'll come over to your place with a VHS video of my friend Phil who recently did a one day gig in Memorial Park in Lansdale and you can be the judge."

Phil had joined in with a pre-formed band that just needed a singer for this one-day gig. They played outdoors in the park on a beautiful summer day and the performance was horrible. The only strong point of that line-up was Phil. I cruised over Scooter's for the first time on a cold fall evening and popped the VHS tape into his VCR. Scooter was very impressed right off the bat. We watched the whole video even though the band's performance was really bad. Scooter was really impressed with the power of Phil's voice. I had told Phil about the power of his voice on Tizzy's lawn several years back. Within a week we all met and agreed to form a band. So Phil and I had to discombobulate all of our equipment from the Rock Room II. Once again we had to deal with all of those confusing wires.

The drum set by this point was big. We had Phil's five-piece set as well as a 3-tom rack of Roto-Toms and a very weird sounding electronic drum that someone just gave to us. I had purchased an electronic drum set made by TAMA and it was called, "Tech-Star." It had realistic feeling drum heads as opposed to all the previous electronic drums that were just hard, rigid, non-feeling plastic. It was a full 5 piece set. By my recollections we had eight or nine cymbals. To get back behind the drums so that you could play you had to smush yourself into the wall and then slide along until you got past the high hat. But, once you got back there you were in a world of percussive joy. Everytime I smushed myself back there and got to see those drums from the drummers viewpoint I paused and allowed the magnificence of the sight to fill my mind. It was a sad deal having to break all that stuff down but we knew that we had found an extremely competent bass player and that it is what our music needed to move on to a new level of exploration.

The place that we played was Scooter's moldy, damp, basement. It wasn't the most comfortable place but it was a place to sweat. We had a couple real serious flooding problems down there as well. Scooter had a very nice Rickenbacker bass. It was a pale yellow color. We officially formed in September 1986. Keep in mind I am honestly trying to become a world famous drummer. I never had lessons. I was self-taught like so many drummers are. If you're gonna get famous you are going to have to work hard and you better be talented. I definitely was talented.

It was obvious I had God given talent. I'll tell you what though, even if you have a God given talent you have to work your ass off to draw it forth. Scooter definitely had a talent to play bass. It may not have appeared that Paul had a God given talent but I can assure you by the time he was running on all cylinders years later you can rest assured it looked like he had worked his God given talent to the surface. He was, after all, the first musician from a non-musical family. That is not an easy thing to do.

In the beginning of this band we were not sounding too good. Phil was having to sing through Scooter's bass amp and that wasn't gonna cut it. Phil had a good voice and we were at the point where something had to be done. So, I made the big move and I bought us a brand-new $1,200 Peavey PA system. I bought it at George's music in Lansdale, Pennsylvania on route 202. We just stepped up in the world. The soundboard of this PA system was like nothing I've ever owned. It was big, heavy, shiny, and had a whole bunch of knobs you could turn. I took about two-dozen pictures of that control board. The PA system came with two big, solid speakers that rose up on big stands. That PA system was so awesome I couldn't believe I owned it. I had to take out a loan to be able to afford it. I had to take a loan out to buy the TAMA Tech Star Electronic drum set as well a few months prior. An old friend of mine, Zam, used to say, "That's gonna help the ball club." Well I'll tell you what. As a result of me purchasing this PA it really helped the ball club. I was really pursuing my dream. Now Phil could sing through a high quality brand-new PA system and he sounded so much better you can't imagine. Scooter got to sing through the PA system as well and I got to have my base drum, snare, and high hat miked. Oh Happy day! When friends came over and saw all of our equipment set up they knew we weren't messin round. Scooter had one good friend who nickname was "Zag." He hung out with us quite a bit and occasionally gave us some observations on our sound here and there. We became a band that played 70% cover tunes and 30% original tunes. Phil's song writing ability at this point was significantly better compared to the old days. He was getting more knowledgeable about everything that had to do with music. Imagine this; he could drum, play guitar, play keyboards, sing, write songs, operate the recording equipment, plug in all the wires and set the levels on our PA system. Damn, all I was, was just a stupid drummer, or was I?

Many years later when Phil and I were barely hanging out with each other anymore, which is hard to believe, he wrote a song lyric that surprised me and really stuck in my heart. He wrote, "Took my best friend's ideas and plans, I had none of my own, and I walk alone." That is powerful and heavy stuff. That was from a song called, "Walk Alone." Phil played it for me one night at his kitchen table and he poured his heart into it. It was very moving. The year was about 1992 and the songs that Phil wrote in those days were very poignant and polished.

I swear to you Phil has written many songs that could have been top 10 hits but it seems that certain things like world stardom are predetermined before birth. Many of the songs created by our next band that we were in together could have easily been top 10 hits. There is no doubt about it. So, getting back to Scooter's basement we got down to serious work. It was the most professional type approach Phil and I had ever been a part of. Scooter knew a lot about music theory and he taught Phil many things.

Since Phil and I were already calling ourselves "By The Way" when we were rocking out in his parent's basement we felt like we still wanted to keep that name because we had numerous original songs and we felt like that we were adding Scooter to our lineup and we wanted to keep our name. I had come up with the name By The Way only because I thought it was a cool conversational phrase. When I had told Phil about the band name idea he was okay with it. We were expecting Scooter to put up a big argument and for it to take days or even weeks to finally decide on a new name but to our total surprise he liked the name "By The Way" and so that's who we were.

Occasionally when Scooter was upstairs grabbing some beers or something Phil would sit down on the drums and play. The drum set was so enormous, sometimes he would just sit there, laugh and laugh and laugh. That drum set made me feel like I was a world famous dude even though I wasn't, yet. After putting a in hard week at work it was glorious to sit down behind my drums while cracking open an ice cold Budweiser.

At one point Scooter got frustrated with Phil's lack of skill on the guitar and I agreed that we needed someone who could play better. Phil was good at playing rhythm while someone else played lead. He was also good at writing his own songs that he could develop from scratch but he wasn't very good with playing hit songs from the radio or other common popular songs. Phil was aware of his shortcoming in that regard and he agreed that we really could use a good guitar player. We auditioned all sorts of people. It was a blast acting like the big guys calling the shots. When people came down the steps and saw our wall of equipment they knew we weren't messin round. We met a couple of good guitarist and we had a lot of good jam sessions. I recorded everything because you never know when magic is going to occur. It was surprising to us that we didn't find anybody who was good enough. We did however get some good recordings of a few RUSH songs with one of Scooter's old friends, Barry.

During this time Scooter kept telling us about an old friend of his whom he's known for a long time. His name was Carl Reggit. He was currently in the Army stationed in Death Valley. Scooter would go on and on about how great he was and how he is in the band as soon as he shows up. Phil and I were like, "Whoa, you can't just declare a guy is in the band." Phil and I told Scooter that were gonna have to meet this guy and decide together whether or not he's getting in the band. Scooter wasn't hearing any of it and he would insist that as soon as Carl got here he was in the band. Carl showed up in the winter around Christmas. He was really skinny and he looked sleep deprived. He was on leave from the Army for the holidays. He was a really easy guy to like. He was always laughing and smiling and was fun to be around. He set up his keyboard and he had a real Moog synthesizer. He had a hard time getting it to work. When he finally got the Moog working it was making sounds that were altering our consciousness. When he finally started playing the keyboard, Phil and I looked at each other and said telepathically, "Holy Shit!" Carl was phenomenal. He was the best musician I'd ever met. He was even better than Brit Kole. When he got done wailing for 10 minutes or so, either Phil or I said, "Oh you are a member of the band for sure!" He busted up laughing. Carl had such an easy smile.

Carl stayed with us for about a month it seems but then had to go back to Death Valley. We recorded all of our jam sessions and I labeled the compilation tape, "Death Valley." Carl could never be a permanent addition to the band because he was in the Army. But, we made him an official member of the band and any time he got leave he could jam with us for sure. When he left, the basement felt empty without him. We were back to a three-piece band that was trying to put together 40 songs so we could call ourselves a top 40 act and get gigs. I said to the guys, "Listen, let's work our asses off and get up to 40 songs so we can get gigs, make money, and get free beer." They agreed. Scooter then added that we could also get chicks. I said, "Oh yes yes, of course, I forgot."

We buckled down and started working on the songs we had been working on. We were playing the Beatles, the Rolling Stones, David Bowie, The WHO, Pink Floyd and we even played a few Monkeys songs. Scooter wanted to play, The Ballad of John and Yoko, so we played that. We also did a good rendition of Lucky Man by ELP. We had about eight original songs that we had perfected. One song was written by Scooter and it was called, "Can You Imagine." Both Phil and I thought it was a really good song. "Can You Imagine" is a perfect example of a song that easily could have been the top 10 radio hit. It was a song that talked about imagining a better world but it was fast and upbeat and really in-your-face. Scooter was, and still is to this day a tremendous Beatles fan. Scooter loves the Beatles to a level that is unhealthy. Scooter has a Beatles collection that is really impressive, to say the least. Somewhere around here Scooter bought a really impressive keyboard. It was a Korg. He could produce sounds from that thing that put us at a whole nother level. He had sound disks that he slide into it and they would produce amazing sounds. He became obsessed with buying as many disks as possible and we had a whole new technology at our fingertips. That's what it was. It was a whole new technology. We had all these new effects to add to our songs.

At one point we auditioned a guitar player and he was great. We got along well with him. He was on time and was dressed nice and was able to carry on a conversation. We told him after three or four jam sessions that we wanted him in the band, which was a big deal for us because we finally found a good guitar player.

He said, "Oh….no thanks, I just want to jam "

I wanted to kill the guy. We never had him back.

It was somewhere around here that Phil started to lose interest. I couldn't believe it. He wanted to quit. I was beside myself. I was fit to be tied. Phil practically had one foot out the door. He was doing a really insane amount of driving in those days. He lived in Lansdale, worked near Catasauqua, and jammed in Sellersville. He was running out of steam. I really couldn't blame him.

I said, "No, No, No."

I convinced him to work together for a goal of one gig. We had been together for seven months and we were close to having four, 45-minute sets of music. We could do a Big Beef-n-Beer. It would be fun for a whole lot of people. It would bring some joy into people's lives. I said to him, "We came this far and we can't quit now." I told him that I would hire a pro to film the gig and to take pictures too. I said to him, "Let's go out in a blaze of Rock 'n Roll glory." He agreed. We decided that we better not tell Scooter. I wasn't sure how Scooter would take the information. I was scared to death that he would just say, "screw it." My heart would have been broken for us to get that far without ever having done a real gig. We actually did do a live show at a little place called the South Perkasie Inn when we really didn't have enough material to do a full show. We all faced our tremendous fears and made it through that show but you really could not call that show a success. I don't think Scooter was scared to death. I was so afraid of walking in the front door to do our show that I thought about running full speed right down the street for a ½ mile or so and then to dart into the woods where no one would find me. It was a cold winter night, which made the escape plan even more insane. I was that scared! I knew I couldn't do that because I would have looked like a fool so I faced my fears and walked right through that door. I could see in Phil's eyes that he was scared to the bone as well. Some of the songs that we played at the South Perk that turned out OK were, "Can You Imagine" (a Scooter original,) "Love in Your Eyes", "Trick Myself"(both Phil originals), "Space Oddity", and "Hide Your Love Away." We also did a good rendition of "Dear Prudence." So technically speaking, this Beef-n-Beer coming up would be our second show. Although it was a pretty crappy and underhand thing to do we didn't tell Scooter that our big gig was going to be our <u>only</u> gig

My plan for global domination was falling far short of the mark. I guess my goal of becoming a world famous drummer will have to wait for the next band I'm in. Perhaps this dream may have to wait for some other life when I live on Karlac, third moon from Theldar. We'll see.

So we continued to work on our songs at Scooter's. We had a single minded goal and we worked very hard at polishing all of our tunes and that we were not going to have any more auditions or jam sessions. We played the same songs over and over again and worked on any weak spots. For me, being the guy who is banging away at the drums, this was all very painful. I drank beer all of the time to help numb the pain in my body. Those guys drank also but they weren't bashing their brains out like I was. We worked on making sure that each song had a perfect beginning, remained tight throughout the song and had a very concise ending.

Week after week we worked like this. I felt more like a professional musician than I had ever felt before. We were all deadly serious and professional because we had that goal in sight. As a result of playing the same songs over and over again we hit another level of cohesion. What we did to make sure we had the show worked out is that we ran through the whole show twice, on different days of course. It was very challenging to say the least and my whole upper body ached from all the drumming. Phil's shirt would be sweaty even though the basement was always very cool. We decided we were ready. Phil had a friend named Kevin at work and Kevin found us a place to play. Kevin was really instrumental in helping us put the show together.

One night on a Sunday when we were rehearsing we had many more hours to go of work, playing. All three of us rarely hung out together. The only time all of us were together was when we were at Scooters, jamming, or partying, or sometimes, rarely, just hanging out. On this particular Sunday it was around dinnertime and we knew that we had to keep rehearsing until about 10 pm in order to maximize our jam time together. I don't think that we ever all went outside to eat food together. I said, "Let's go up to the Keystone Diner and sit down and eat a meal together like civilized people for once." They both bought it. So we hopped in Phil's car, probably, and drove to the Keystone Diner, which is one of those old fashioned restaurants where everything taste like Grandma made it. So we got a booth and ordered and we each got coffee because we all needed a kick because we knew we had about 4 hours of "working" ahead of us.

Something magical happened to me in that booth because I became aware of this feeling for the first time in my life, ever. I felt like a "REAL" musician who was in a band. There was something about us 3 sitting there and we all looked a bit tired and we were taking a break from this constant rehearsing and neither one of us had much to say and it was so real. When I was growing up you would always see pictures of musicians in the Rolling Stone magazine and they would be at a bus stop, sitting in a hotel lobby, or sitting at a bar looking tired and worn out. Well I got that vibe from us guys in "By The Way" sitting in a booth at the Keystone Diner in Sellersville, Pennsylvania. The feeling lingered and I drank in every moment of it.

Here is a spooky twist of fate. Guess where our gig was held? It was held in a small hall that was two hundred feet from where my dad had lived and died, Melody Lakes Park. When I found out that we were playing there I had one of those eerie, spooky, creepy type feelings whereby you see that sometimes things in life go full circle. Here I was finally playing a real gig and it was going to be within eyesight of where my musician father had died and his musician son had come back to where his spirit passed from this earth. My dad died in his bed. Scary kids!!! When I used to visit my Dad I used to shoot pool in that little building. I'm sure that Phil and I shot pool there many years before. The day we got there and had to set up all of our equipment and all of those wires (This Cunfusion,Wires) I walked over to my dad's old mobile home. It looked completely different but I really did feel that some of his spirit was visiting this area for our gig. He was going to be one of the guiding Angels watching over our happening.

Nighttime rolled around and the people began to show up. It had taken us about five hours to set everything up. Everybody had bought tickets days and weeks in advance. It was 10 bucks per person. It was a Beef-n-Beer; all you can eat and drink. We had five ½ kegs of Budweiser and Phil's younger brother Tom ran the food side of the event. He did a really good job too. The roast beef sandwiches melted in your mouth. There was enough potato salad and coleslaw to feed an army. We had 110 people who had bought tickets and maybe another 20 or more people showed up at the door. Those rock 'n roll animals polished off every speck of food and drank all five kegs even before the last set was over. We also had a raffle for a bottle of Brut Champagne and Cuervo Gold Tequila. The winners shared with everybody and those bottles were polished off in no time. This was one fired up audience. A few of the songs that we absolutely nailed were Lucky Man, Go Ask Alice, Saw Her Standing There, Steppin Stone, For your Love by the Yardbirds, Mary Mary, I'm a Believer, Can't Explain, The Kids are Alright, My Generation, I Can See for Miles, and Can You Imagine. During the 2nd set we played "Go Ask Alice" and Phil decided to not play his guitar. He had a cool helicopter sound on his keyboard that brought back memories of the 1970's Huey Helicopters that were so prevalent in the

Vietnam war and that added a subliminal element to the song I think. So it was just Scooter on his bass, me on drums, and Phil singing. We brought the house down on that song. The people cheered really loudly and then there was a pause and the crowd started to yell and cheer again and it turned into a roar! It was so loud that it actually frightened me. It was this wall of screaming and it triggered a primal fear within me. Phil and Scooter and I all looked at each other and said telepathically, "Holy Shit". The crowd had gone bat shit crazy!

During the final set we played "For Your Love" note for note perfect and I nailed the drum track. There was a lot of Roto-Tom in that song and I didn't miss one note. I was so happy when I heard the playback late that night and realized that I didn't hit any rim shots. I had asked the video camera guy to move all the way to the back of the hall so that a good shot of all of the people dancing could be seen. It turned out to be a really good idea on my part. The people went bonkers on that song. A mosh pit broke out and people started to slam into each other and jump around like hooligans. I certainly had achieved my goal of being a drummer in a band that had a gig where people danced their asses off had a really good time and forgot about all of their worries. It sure is a lot of hard work bringing your dreams to fruition. At one point during the second set when my nerves had calmed down to the point that I no longer felt like I was about to die I looked out at the audience and the whole dance floor was full of people dancing and smiling. We played so many simple, straight four beat songs that it was really easy for the people to dance and have a good time. The dance floor was literally full the whole night.

We started playing at 8 PM so that we could be done by midnight. We were playing smack-dab on the edge of a whole neighborhood of mostly senior citizens so we couldn't push it too far. We did have a complaint from one of the important neighbors but they let us finish our songs. We crushed the already worn out audience with three WHO songs. The last song we did was, "I Can See for Miles" and we obliterated that song and we did an extended massive rock star ending that brought the house down. Phil climbed up on a small ledge and came jumping down off of it to crush the final cord into the ground. What a mother flipping blast!!!

The big gig was over and Phil and I knew that the band was finished. It was a wild scene. When I tried to stand up I fell back down, backwards, onto the drum throne because I was so exhausted. I couldn't stand up. I had to sit there for a few minutes. I needed to inhale a couple of beers to get my head right. The band had a top-secret cooler of icy cold beers. We had worked hard and achieved our goal. We were all so exhausted that we had to leave our equipment there and Kevin locked up. We all met the next morning to pick up our gear and it was weird to know that, "By The Way" was no more.

I called Scooter and told him that Phil wanted to quit and that he was too exhausted to go on and that I wanted to quit too. Scooter was not a happy camper. He was pissed off but it didn't take him long to calm down; I would say two weeks. I drove up there about a week later and he was busy on projects around his house. I actually think he was a bit relieved that the whole thing was over because it took up so much of all of our time. I maintained a good friendship with Scooter for many years. We actually did a few musical projects together. I actually got to jam with Carl and Scooter together one time. They were working on 6 songs that they were going to record in the studio with this guy George Lamdo. I learned all 6 songs and wowed them down in Scooter's basement. Carl was blown away that I put in that much preparation time. This was in 1990 or 91. They all agreed that I was hired but we never went into the studio. I was very disappointed. Such is life. I am still in touch with Scooter now and again. Phil and Scooter on the other hand, never talked again.

CHAPTER SEVEN

THIRD FLOOR

Now we get down to the meat of the matter. Now we get down to the real deal.

Now we go,
   Up the stairs,
    Up the stairs,
     To the Third Floor
      To the Third Floor.

Since "By The Way" had completed that big goal of a live show Beef-n-Beer and it was a success and many people had a total blast I felt like I had finally achieved my dream, to feel like a real drummer. I had finally done what I had seen other drummers, who I considered to be real drummers, do, and that was put on a live show. There was a complete change in my inner demeanor. I felt different. I felt like I had gotten a monkey off my back. I had joy in my heart for a change. I was happier in my day-to-day existence. I had the video of the gig to watch, the pictures to look at and the boombox recording to listen to. The boombox recording turned out really well. I gave both Phil and Scooter a copy of the video and all of the pictures as a gift. Those two dudes were the guys who helped me achieve a big goal in my life.

As the months went by I started to get bored again. Phil and I continued to jam as we had set up shop in the Rock Room II again but I could tell he was sick of our same old songs. I started to say, over and over again, we have to form another band. We had so much experience and momentum we couldn't just stop. I told him I'll go crazy if we can't find some good musicians to work with, to form a whole new soundscape. He wasn't quite as hungry as I was because after all when he was a kid he wasn't obsessed with music, drumming, and wanting to be in a band. I just kept saying it over and over again, "We have to form another band." Some times I said it under my breath in an almost trance like state. Phil eventually had to tell me to, "Shut the Fuck up."

We did the customary thing people did in those days. We put a free ad in the "Trade-in-Times." It was a small ad magazine that you could use to buy or sell stuff or post job openings or offer your services. It was free. It was also on an honor system. If you sold your item you were supposed to send in 10% of your profit or whatever you felt was a reasonable sum. We advertised something along these lines. Paul probably wrote up the ad because he was good at writing.

"Drummer with good equipment and singer/ songwriter/ guitar player with keyboard and Peavey PA system looking to form professional band with guitar player, bass player, and keyboard player."

I can't remember how long it took and for the life of me I can't remember what month we met but I remember it was a cool evening and I am pretty sure it was late August and it was definitely 1987. That is a night I often think back to because it was the beginning of something that was magical. I would love to write a detailed and thorough telling of the story of Third Floor but that is not the purpose of this book. I'm going to give some detail though so that the reader can understand why I was so enamored with the phrase Third Floor and why it was so dear to my heart. Phil and I got a response from some guys in Norristown. Phil actually took the call and called me to tell me about it. We met those guys at Phil's parent's house. We saw their headlights and went out to meet them. The bigger guy with incredibly long brownish hair was Sam, and the younger looking guy wearing a blue denim jacket was Garret. We stood outside and spoke briefly and agreed we should go inside, plug-in, and see what happens. Sam used Phil's keyboard and Garret had his red guitar. It wasn't on fire, quite yet. Phil didn't play guitar that night; he focused on singing. The only song I remember us playing was a Jimi Hendrix song. We played our way through bits and pieces of many songs. Phil and I could tell immediately that these guys were good and that they knew their stuff. Hopefully they thought the same thing of us. It was kind of interesting in that Phil's youngest brother Blaine was there, sitting on the bottom steps and his good friend Gary Kole was there as well. If you remember, those guys first met and became buddies during the, "On The Rocks" era.

Phil, Garret, Sam, and I went up to the kitchen table and we all talked about our own years of experience and what our goals were. I remember distinctly saying that I had only done three gigs so far and I wanted to do a whole lot more. I remember saying that I felt like I had been playing my whole life and now I was at the age that I could really get out and do professional gigs all the time. I told those guys that Phil had a lot of original song ideas and he wanted to hear his songs played with a full band plus he wanted to rock. From listening to Garret and Sam you could tell that they were both very knowledgeable musicians. Sam was going to college for music for God's sake. Sam was the first person I had ever met who was going to college for music. Sam was advanced in his knowledge of music theory compared to most keyboard players you meet. Sam was also a singer. He could hit all the notes. We learned from Garret that he was obsessed with playing the guitar. Garret was young but he was very serious. Turns out he could also play the mandolin. I don't think he told us that night but he taught music lessons to many, many students. We hung out at the kitchen table and talked for over an hour. No one was home at the time so we had control of the place. We were all drinking beer and none of us even thought about it but Garret was under age. We all agreed that it was a good meeting and that we should get together and jam some more. Nobody said anything about us agreeing that we were a band.

Little did we know what the fates had in store for us!

Within a few weeks Phil and I took some of our stuff to Sam's parents house in Norristown. Those guys told us there was more room there than Phil's basement and they were right. We were down in the cellar, as usual. We jammed together several times and we eventually all agreed that we were a band. I was so happy that they agreed because I could tell that Garret really knew how to play the guitar. He was a life long committed guitar player whereas Phil didn't start playing until his second year of college. There was no comparison between the two guys. When Garret did Led Zeppelin riffs, RUSH riffs or WHO riffs, it sounded like one of those rock legends was in the room with you. He was really talented.

When I was in high school I was in a band, if you want to call it that, and we played one song for our school's once a year production of the Gong Show. We had this girl who had played piano her whole life. The other girl in the band who was a friend of mine Lori G. said one day, "We got it made because we have keyboards." I don't know why but for some reason that phrase stuck with me. We played Jessica by the Allman Brothers and got gonged because it was too long of a song. At least the very talented piano player girl, whose name I do not remember, got to play her whole piano solo. She was classically trained all of her life and it showed. Now that I was in this brand new band and we had Sam on keys I knew we had it made because he knew every chord ever written and his keyboards would be a solid foundation to hold the songs together. Plus he could sing really well and would be able to harmonize with Phil. I figured that Phil was going to play rhythm guitar but that never happened. He focused 100% on vocals and lyrics and I never knew what went down such that those guys decided that Phil wasn't going to play guitar at all.

Since Phil knew how to drum and I knew that it would be really hard for me to play four, 45 minute sets per night on top of all of the rehearsing, carrying our equipment all over the place, while also working a difficult full-time job, I decided it would be a good idea to let Phil play four or five songs per gig. These would be songs that Phil played specifically. They would be songs that I had nothing to do with. It turned out to be a good idea in the long run. We sort of became a band that had a band within it. People really enjoyed seeing Phil and I switch up on the drums because they really liked the songs that Phil played on. Garret ended up writing real bluesy songs for Phil to play the drums on. One song that became a real house pleaser was, "One Foot Out the Door."

The one problem we still had though was that we didn't have a bass player. You can't have a band without a bass player! Well, those guys, Garret and Sam told us that they knew a bass player and that he was going to be, "The Guy" and that was all there was to it. They said there was no need to audition anybody. Phil and I said, "OK, OK," we figured if he was as good as Garret and Sam he would be worth the wait. His name was Sigonz. I said hez, zoh, what? They said, "Sigonz." I said "what" and they said his name again. I said, "What the hell kind of name is that?" They said, "That's his name." Phil also spoke up and pretty much said in so many words, that is really weird. We asked them how it was spelled and then we practiced saying his name. I then asked so what is his last name. They said that he doesn't have one. So I said, "You mean to tell me he's a one name person, like Bono, Cher, Madonna, and Sting, stuff like that?" They said "Yup!" I said to Phil, "do you believe this, this is unbelievable." That was that and so this Sigonz guy was going to be our bass player and we pretty much had to wait until he showed up. (*Don't tell anybody but I secretly thought it was totally cool that we had a one name guy in the band.*)

It was right around this time frame that I was enjoying RUSH's new album called "Hold Your Fire" also known as the RED Album. I had always felt like I was on a mission to one day end up in a great band. As you know I had my dream to one day be a great drummer. Well there was one lyric in one of the songs that really stuck with me. The name of the song is "Mission." The lyric is as follows.....

A Spirit with a Vision
Is a dream with a mission

I felt like those few words explained accurately what I was up to. At first Phil wasn't really diggin the lyric but one day, up in my tiny apartment while we were listening to the album he finally got the meaning and thought it was an accurate description of my constant striving.

Phil, Sam, Garret and I, continued to jam except we were working on songs now, no jamming. We all had the same goal of becoming a good local band and to play gigs everywhere. One of my biggest motivations as a young Irishman was free beer. I was obsessed with consuming beer just about every moment of the day when I was not at work. Garret, although he was a young man, enjoyed that idea tremendously. You see he had the same Irish DNA as I. The problem though was that we had to wait for Sigonz to show up. One day Phil or I got really frustrated and asked how long is this guy going to be away. Garret answered about six months. Phil and I pretty much flipped out. We yelled, "Six months!" We were both fit to be tied. They said yep. I couldn't believe it. They were both still insisting we wait for this damn bass player. Some of the time had already passed so maybe now we only had to wait three months. I remember thinking to myself, this guy better be a God damn good musician.

Numerous days when we were practicing in Sam's parents house Mrs. R. would flick the light switch signaling it was time to stop playing. At first this didn't bother me. All it took was a few more times and I shouted at those guys outside that this can't go on anymore. I told them that I really wanted to some day be a professional drummer and getting world famous wouldn't be such a bad idea. We were all on the same page as far as that was concerned. I told them, "We have to find our own place." They all agreed. I had seen hundreds of TV shows and movies where totally cool people in New York City had their own flats, as they called them, in some old warehouse somewhere. That's what I wanted. I told those guys we had to find a big place in an old warehouse where we could be a real band and have a totally cool hang out as well. It was, "YES" all around from my new band mates. Amazingly it didn't take us long to find a third floor "flat" in a building that had a carpet business on the first floor and was only a few miles from Sam's parents house. As soon as we saw the place we wanted it. The name of the company in which our new space was in was, "Wall Coverings Ltd." Our new place was in the little town called Bridgeport, Bridgeport Pennsylvania. The rent was $300 per month and when Sigonz eventually arrived that would be $60 per month per guy, which would be totally easy for each of us to pay. We were in baby, we were in. Sure.

The energy of our rehearsals was totally different in our new space. We were no longer the boys practicing in the basement. We were now the musicians rehearsing in our flat. It was so much cooler and we felt totally hip. We had a bathroom so we could drink and drink and drink. Phil and Sam could smoke cigarettes to their hearts delight. We moved in there in late fall, early winter and we soon found out that we had no heat so we froze our asses off. It didn't stop us. Nothing could stop us. There are a great many tales I could tell but I have to keep focused on getting to the purpose of this book, which is the "Third Floor Movie Mystery."

The day finally arrived when our bass player showed up. We first met him outside of Sam's house. I met him on the street. He could have been a tall lanky looking dude with long hair and a big nose but he wasn't. He was a streamlined looking cat with short black hair and intelligent eyes. He was a man of few words. I remember staring at him and thinking,

"I hope this son of a bitch was worth the wait." Guess what? He was! He could really play and was super smart. He was like Garret and Sam. He knew music theory inside and out. You could tell those three were all friends. Garret and Sam brought Sigonz up to speed quickly. Sigonz absorbed the information faster than any musician I had ever met. It turns out that what Sigonz was doing while he was away in the New York was teaching and taking courses in classical guitar. The guy could play classical guitar, as far as I'm concerned, like a world-class player. I'm not exaggerating. So here the last puzzle piece to the band is a bass player who, in the next few months, got a Masters degree in classical guitar. Do you believe that? It is absolutely, positively, mind-boggling. We were all invited to his Master's Thesis whereby he performed and it is safe to say that Phil and I had never seen anything like that in our lives. We were all humbled by his performance. All through out the whole history of our band I never called Sigonz by his proper name. It turns out he had a proper name and it was Mitchell Sibbines.

One day while Phil and I were cleaning out some of the old junk that was up in our studio/ warehouse place I stumbled upon this large sturdy cardboard sign that said, "Men's / Women's Third Floor." That's all it said. It didn't say "Men's / Women's Restrooms Third Floor." It was a strange sign and it was really old so we decided to keep it. I said something like this old sign can be our mascot type thing. I said that we should totally keep the sign and show it to people. It was a good "Conversation Piece." I was up in the rafters above the bathroom because there was a large exhaust fan up there and it had no insulation in it. Phil climbed up into the rafters as well to help clear out old junk. In the first few weeks of being there the police kept coming up and banging on our door. Some of us were often smoking pot up there as musicians do and we couldn't keep having cops banging on our door. Garret's guitar was so loud that its sound was carrying out across the neighborhood. We had to do something about it so I was up there shoving big pieces of foam into the fan structure to cut down on the sound so that it couldn't travel as far. It worked. People stopped calling the cops so often. We also did something very smart to help alleviate this problem of people calling the cops. Phil typed up a very professionally written letter explaining who we were as a band and what we were doing. It described how we were serious musicians that were working on our act so that we could get out there and start working. We walked around the small neighborhood of brown brick row houses and put a letter into about every fourth mailbox or so. We knew the word would spread throughout the tight knit neighborhood. The people who lived in that little Bridgeport neighborhood believed us, and the complaints stopped.

We the guys of Third Floor drank a lot of beer. We drank insane amounts of beer. Our beer of choice was Budweiser. Sigonz drank the least amount of beer. He would occasionally show up with a case of Heineken on Friday or Saturday night and it tasted so good after having drank about 300 Budweisers in a row. We all would show up with cases except Garret because, you're not going to believe this, he was only 19 when the band was formed. Phil and I were 25 while Sam and Sigonz were 22. We would polish off our beer all of the time and someone would have to walk the one block to the bar around the corner. We gave that bar so much business in the 2 ¼ years we were together it is astonishing. The name of the bar was Rossi's. One day when I was voted against I walked out to get two "Tall Boy" six-packs of Budweiser. We used to say in those days as, "Ya'll Fly!" Then someone would say, "Oh no, Ya'll Fly!" This would go on for five minutes then someone would say, "No, I decided, Ya'll Fly!" Eventually someone would give in and it seemed like it was usually me although I think we all did our fair share of running out to get beer. Inevitably when I was walking over to the bar I would end up singing, "Fly by Night" the RUSH song.

We had been discussing what our band name should be before I walked out the door to go get more beer. I know Phil and Sam were there and I think Garret was there also. They were looking at that old sign. I know I was throwing out some band names that I was pretty strong about. Picking a band name when there are five guys in the band is almost impossible. Somebody is going to get their toes stepped on. There is no two ways about it. By the time I came back those guys had decided we were going to be "Third Floor." I said something like, "What…..that is the stupidest thing I've ever heard." I was serious. I thought maybe they were joking me and so after five minutes I said, "OK, the joke is over, good one, now let's get serious." But, they were serious. They pointed out that we were on the Third Floor, that I had found that strange old sign and that we all wanted to get a cool flat in an old warehouse so why not call ourselves Third Floor. After I thought about it for a while it did seem kind of cool. I started to like the idea and once I was sure those guys weren't kidding me I said, "OK, We're

Third Floor." I don't know what Sigonz thought of the name. He often was not around because he lived all the way down in the city. Someone must have told him over the phone.

Once we gelled with Sigonz there was a no stopping us. We could learn new songs so quickly it blew my mind. We were writing new songs, original songs, that seemed to me that we all knew the song before it was even explained to us. Garret and Sigonz were the principal writers of our original songs. I once complained about how Phil had songs to offer and that we should add some of his songs, which were really our songs, Phil's, and mine but this idea fell on deaf ears. I couldn't believe it. However, Phil's ideas on how to shape and mold songs were taken seriously by Garret, Sigonz, and Sam. Phil didn't play any guitar during the whole Third Floor era. I thought this was really un- believable. He did eventually play guitar again after Third Floor broke up. I had many jam sessions with him for years after Third Floor was no more and he developed significant guitar playing chops. I mean he could really shred on acoustic guitar. Sam obviously also got his opinions heard as well. Sam became a mentor to Phil's vocals. Sam's mom was a voice teacher and so Sam was an expert in this area. As a result of Garret's persistent insistence Phil eventually took vocal lessons from a person whose name I think was Jerry. Phil became Mr. deadly serious singer guy. There is one thing I failed to mention and that is that Sigonz could also sing. He ended with a couple of songs that he sang lead vocal on. As time went by with Garret singing bits and pieces of backing vocals his voice got stronger as well. Months down the road he also got to the point were he was singing lead on a few songs. I would say that it was about 6 months after Sigonz had arrived that those guys were working on 3 and sometime 4 part harmonies that were flawless. You could have knocked me over with a feather. There was one particular day when we were playing and it hit me during the song that we were incredibly good. When some of our songs would end we all would look at each other while the amps droned and the cymbal sizzles dimmed and we were all thinking in our minds, "Oh dear Lord, we are Rock Gods of the Universe." You could also feel this special magic energy hanging in the air. It was there, it was really there, you could feel it. I knew that we had something really special.

It got to the point that Garret was starting to take over practices about a year down the road with barking out orders and such. He often took over practice, I mean rehearsal, and kept us working and focusing on our problems. Phil was also vocal as far as what songs we should work on. I was the drummer and I was so thrilled to be in a band that good I was happy to work on what ever they wanted to work on. Sam came up with all of his own keyboard sounds for each song. He eventually bought this amazing keyboard that had weighted keys like a piano but yet had a computer brain with 1001 sounds. Sigonz was quiet and reserved and was totally professional. When he did speak up everybody listened.

One day at rehearsal there is this slick looking guy with short curly blonde hair there. I am introduced to him. He was there about 2 months after Sigonz had showed up. He is Allen Newe and he is a sax player that Sam knew from college. I'm thinking to myself, "Holy crap, we have a sax player now?" We started rehearsing some of our songs while Garret and Sam tell him what notes to play and he starts in with no problem. After three or four weeks we were blasting away and it's time for one of his songs and he starts tearing through on his bits that he composed for himself. I remember this moment because for me so much of playing in a band as a drummer is sweating bullets and now I've got this awesome sax player who shows up out of nowhere and is adding this incredible element to our already smoking hot band. I looked right at him as he was 4 feet away and I could not get over the fact that I was in a band with a sax player who could wail. It was all too much; too much in a good way. For me to say I was happy would be an understatement. I found it hard to believe that Phil and I went from trying like hell to find good musicians while with Scooter up in Sellersville to finding four brilliant musicians that were beyond my wildest expectations.

Some of the songs we had perfected were cover songs "White Room", "World Turning", "Who do you Love", "Satisfaction Guaranteed", "South Central Rain", "Fire" and "Crazy" by REM, "Desire" our legendary cover of our "Doors" medley and our ever expanding expression of "Low Spark of High Heeled Boys". The names of our high quality original songs are, "Today", Smile (wait and see)", "Broke Again", "Den of Inequity", "Nine Lives", "Closing Right Up", "Visions of Color", "Up & Down", "Tragedy", "City Lights", "Obstacles", "Shuffling", "Attraction", "Rememberin-some-fun", "One Foot Out the Door", "Lonely Girl" "Bananas and Ice Tea" and many other tunes. It is an honest-to-goodness shame that we didn't become world famous.

Chapter Eight
OUR FIRST GIG AND BEYOND

Third Floor didn't do its first gig outside of our studio warehouse for one year and four months. We did our first gig at a VFW Hall on 2nd Street in Lansdale, PA. my hometown, on December 3rd 1988. Due to the fact that we were young creative people and we wanted to be different, Garret or I said we shouldn't have a studio we should have a studea. We had to be different. So if you were a Third Floor insider you knew we had a Studea warehouse. I booked this gig because I couldn't take the delays anymore. Garret was an intense perfectionist. He wanted every song to be perfect. I knew from filling in on drums for a tribute band called "Tribute" for two nights in the summer of 87 that played top 40 hits and old songs that we were better than any bands out there. So I booked the gig and the other guys all agreed that we were ready to go. Technically speaking Third Floor had done a gig or two on South Street before this Beef-n-Beer but they were one-hour gigs on weeknights when people in the bar barely paid attention to you. This gig at the VFW was going to be important because we knew we had more than enough material to cover four hours of time. Speaking of encores we had to do multiple encores that night. I told Garret that I had read countless times that all sorts of world famous bands said that getting out and playing live is the best way to get better. You have to get out there in front of audiences and play your guts out to every audience like it's your last gig ever. The gig was another Beef-n-Beer but they limited the number of kegs to two, I think. They had a bar there so people could get their drinks at the bar. Phil's younger brother, Tom, whom had done the food for the Beef-n-Beer for the "By The Way" did the food for this gig as well and once again he did a fantastic job. Phil's youngest brother Blaine was at this gig along with all of his friends, many of who were also at the "By The Way" gig. People were on the dance floor dancing like crazy practically from the start. Our fans from several Third Floor Studea parties were clearly familiar with our songs. I lay down such rock solid beat and all the other guys play so well we had people dancing even though it was their first time seeing us. Some of the locals saw all of the cars parked everywhere and they came in to see the show. Once again I was so nervous that I had to work hard on not bursting into flames. I stayed very nervous for the whole first set of 45 minutes or so. So here I am, now a grown man, fulfilling the little Roslyn boy's dream to play music to a bunch of people and for them to forget their worries and to go out on the dance floor and to dance their cares away. Me and my mates, in the band, were fulfilling the young child's dream. We had every person at that gig having a total blast. Garret's red guitar was on fire for sure that night. Garret's red guitar was on fire on many a night!

I can't write another sentence without mentioning our two roadies. We had two roadies who were friends with the Norristown guys all through high school. Their names were Allen Thenn and LML. Yep, here we go again with another guy with a nickname. I called LML, LML all the time. No one called him by his proper name. As months went by from the time I had first met him I finally said enough already what is this guy's Christian name? So they told me his name was Matt Lenor and that people had always called him little Matt when he was growing up because he was always so pint sized. One day somebody along the way called him LML, which stood for Little Matt Lenor and it stuck. So from that point on everybody called him LML. I always called him LML. How strange is it that our saxophone player's name was Allen Newe and we had a roadie whose name was Allen Thenn? Is that not one of the most unbelievable coincidences? It has to be. I mean wow, that is really strange.

Both Allen, who was tall and lanky, and LML were at practically every single rehearsal. I am not kidding about this. They were there constantly. It was like they were both members of the band. They both learned how to operate our soundboard or PA system. As the months turned to years neither one of those guys quit. They stayed with us the whole way. By the time we did our first gig at the VFW we had a very impressive amount of equipment. Garret had bought a second guitar amp so that his guitar could always cut through all of the sound especially on his guitar solos. I had this gig videotaped because I knew it was going to be very special. I was right and I was so smart to think ahead on this and it doesn't bother me one bit that I paid one of the their Norristown friends $100 to do the job. I had a couple copies made to give out to people in the band.

We really were one of the best bands around. We started out opening for bands but we only did that three or four times before we became the main act. There were times down the road when we managed to get into a new bar and we had to play the opening role once again. We would only play for an hour but the owner of the place or the manager on duty could see and hear how good we were and we would be booked as the main act in the future. We were not as good or as popular as Beru Revue for instance. The show they put on was amazing. They hit you with song after song and never let you catch your breath. Phil and I started seeing Beru Revue as soon as we turned 21 back in 1983 at the Ambler Cabaret again and again. This was years before we ever met our future Norristown band mates. There was another band that I had seen in those days that was a well-oiled machine and that was LeCompt. We played the Red Garter Inn during the same time they did in 1989. Those guys toured up-and-down the eastern seaboard so we were not in their league in that regard. The Red Garter was on Baltimore Avenue in Clifton Heights. They were extremely professional but they played popular radio music of that era. Third Floor was way more of an original blues band then we were a cover band. I'm sure those guys had original music also. They had a really good drummer. I sat next to him at a Terry Bozio (Missing Persons) drum clinic at George's Music once. One night Phil, Sam and I went down to the Red Garter to check it out. We wanted to see if it was the type of place that we would like to play. We decided that it would be a really nice place to do gigs at and so Phil and Sam spoke to the manager that night to try to work our band into their schedule. Le Compt was playing that night and they were really good. A band that we shared the stage with that was also very good was Sinclair. Sinclair was the band who was responsible for getting us our first gig in the Ambler Cabaret, which was so important to Phil and I because we used to see Beru Revue there and we dreamed of one day playing that venue. I will always be thankful to Sinclair for helping us get our first gig at the Ambler Cabaret. Third Floor opened for Sinclair one night at Dewar's Tavern in the Willow Grove area. I had to play on their drummers over sized Ludwig kit and it was a trip for me. The lead singer and guitar player of Sinclair are the backbone of the Legendary American Led Zeppelin Tribute band, "Get the Led Out." I've seen their act 3 times at different venues but since I've been so broke lately I haven't been able to see more shows. If you haven't seen "Get The Led Out" you don't know what you're missing. You've really got to get out there and see those guys. The most insane drummer I ever saw was the drummer from "Gasoline." I got to play on his drums at an outdoor show in Towamencin Park. That guy drummed like his soul was on fire. I've never seen anything like it before, or since. Another good band from back in the day in the mid 1980's was Tommy Comwell and the Young Rumblers. I once saw Tommy Comwell walk across the bar at the Ambler Cabaret while all of the people had their drinks there while he was playing a blistering guitar lead. I looked right up at him, right into his eyes, as he continued to shread. I said to myself under my breath, "Holy Shit." Not only did he not spill a single drink but, he didn't even bump one of those little straws that lean out of the drinks.

One night was particularly special for Phil and I. We were playing the Ambler Cabaret on October 6th, 1989. I didn't expect anything different to occur that evening. Little did I know what I was in for. As we are there waiting for our time to run up on stage I see a guy that looks like Bob Beru. Holy Shit, it is Bob Beru! He was there doing work for Steve Mountain Management. I could not believe my eyes. Phil and I tripped all over ourselves trying to maintain our cool. We asked him if he was going to stay to hear us play and we reminded him of what huge fans we had always been of his. Well guess what sports fans, he stayed! We got to play for Himself. When Phil and I got up on the stage, the Ambler stage, where we had seen Beru Revue so many times and had dreamed of one day being Rocker's ourselves, well it was just too much.

We, the guys in Third Floor, were together over two years and we saw a lot of bands that were not very good at all. It just goes to show you how hard it is to be in a good band and how hard it is to find that priceless collection of people that can form a really tight knit unit. We were so lucky and as I have said before there were times I could not believe that I was in a lineup of such awesome musicians.

Since this book is not supposed to be a history of Third Floor I can't name all of the local fans and supporters. I have to mention Daisy who was Garret's girlfriend. Garret was lucky to have Daisy on his arm. There was a guy name Shaster who I want to mention because he recorded a few of our gigs and he was a good fan. He made a recording of us that was the best recording to date. It became known as the Shaster Boot. There was also Karen, who was a good fan, and she ended up dating and then going steady with Shaster. There was also a lady who, it seems, was at every gig. She had long flowing black hair and she had an unusual dance style and she was out there dancing to almost every darn song. What a fan she was! God bless her, she was such a good fan of our band. Her name was Karen and I will never forget her. Her boyfriend was Mitchell Schiffen. He was a tall guy with a dark beard. Karen and Mitchell moved to Minnesota to find work. There was this other chick that was a fan and her name was Danice. She had black hair and ended up dating Allen our roadie. She was always hanging around. Phil's youngest brother Blaine was a regular fixture at almost all of our gigs. He was a fan of the band. LML had a buddy, Sam Schuman who was at a lot of our gigs. Sam had a nice pool table in his basement. He was dressed as a surgeon at the first Third Floor Halloween Party.

On a side note I saved Shaster's life. He is the only person who's life I have saved. We were at one of our legendary Third Floor parties and were done playing and every one was still hanging out until very late. Phil, Sam, and I used to stay up until the tweety birds used to come out. On this particular night we were just hanging out and all of a sudden Shaster started to act strange. He was moving around frantically and then he started to point at his throat. I asked him, "Are you choking?" He said yes by nodding his head up and down. I put my arms around him and made my hands into one fist and jammed them up under his rib cage at the top of his stomach. I pulled with all my might 1, 2, 3 times and nothing happened. Someone said, "What the hell is Dan doing to Shaster"? Other people looked over and thought I was messing around and thought what I was doing looked awful and stupid.

I jumped around to look at his face and to look at his eyes. He had a look of shear terror in his eyes. He couldn't do any thing. He couldn't nod up and down or point to his throat. He stood there frozen and all of the communication came from his eyes and he was terrified. I jumped back behind him and with all of the might I could summon and with making absolutely sure my balled up fist of both hands clasped together was in the soft flesh at the top of his belly, right underneath his rib cage I gave 1, 2 mighty tugs inward and then a loud "whoop" was heard and a shot of something flew, I kid you not, 20 feet in the air and then bounced another 5 feet.

Shaster doubled over and I thought he was going to puke but he just gasped for air for a couple breaths and he stayed doubled over for 2 minutes or so. He was trying to regain his equilibrium. He just had the fear of death put in him. People stood around and were speechless then everybody starting clapping and patting me on the back and Shaster stood up and thanked me again and again. People started hugging Shaster and the whole party rebooted. I couldn't believe how hard I had to grab at him to get that food out. Someone picked up the piece of food and it was a piece of pizza crust. That is why it was so damned hard to get out of there.

I would be re-miss in my duties if I did not tell the tale of Mr. Harry Johnstone. Mr. Harry Johnstone was a senior citizen. He was a black man. He was a man of modest means but he was a proud man. He always wore a suit with a nice hat like the gentleman wore back when men had honor and when men were polite. Mr. Harry Johnstone was a classy man. Our young Garret picked him up one day hitch hiking. Back in Harry's day a man had no problem with sticking out his thumb for a ride. Garret showed Harry our Studea and those two hung out together up there when it was cold outside. Harry was about 70 years old and he looked it. But, it turns out he could hold a tune. Garret showed Harry a few tunes and the next thing you know those guys are working out songs together. It was totally surprising. Who knew?

Harry lived pretty far away. He lived down in West Chester. So he showed up now and again but when he did Garret and him would work out there bits during the day when everybody else was at work or school. It got to the point were those two had 4 or 5 numbers down. They were good too. These were heavy blues tunes. Mr. Harry Johnstone knew about the blues. Our young Garret, although he was a white boy from suburbia, had the soul of an old blues guitarist.

Mr. Johnstone performed with us at the VFW gig in Lansdale. He could really sing. Sometimes it was hard to figure out his lyrics but the people loved him. In one song he renamed our band. He said that, "They used to be the Third Floor but now we called the Roof Rockers!"

Mr. Harry Johnstone was such a character. The one song he sang that night that Garret and him put together was "Done Got Over" and the crowd loved it. We also played a song called "Conversation Piece." He stayed at my place twice when it was way too late for me to drive him home after two different gigs. I treated him to breakfast at the legendary Astor Diner in North Wales. I treated him to two shots of Gin after he finished his breakfast and I saw a look of total contentment on his face as we began the long drive home to his place around 1 in the afternoon.

Harry is up in Heaven right now but I will never forget him.

There was this other character in the neighborhood who was a total trip. The guys in the band had told me about this local guy whose name was "Dude Man." His name was "Dude Man" because every time he opened his mouth he said, dude man. I said to the guys, "That's completely ridiculous. There can't be a guy who constantly says dude man."

They said, "Oh yes there is. Every time he says something he has to include the phrase dude man."

I replied by saying, "Well I don't doubt that he occasionally says dude man, but there is no way he says dude man all the time."

Garret got angry at me. It was very easy for Garret to get angry. Him and I used to get angry at each other all the time. So Garret says to me, "I'm going to bring him around and you can see for yourself."

"Okay, okay" I said. "Bring him around and I'll see for myself."

I guess a couple of days went by and some of my band mates and I were standing around this bar we had that was covered with white Formica or one of those surfaces, and in walks Garret with this kind of short looking guy.

They walked towards us and the guy says to me, "Dude Man, are you the drummer?"

I said, "Yes I am."

He says, "Yo dude man, I'm Dude Man."

I said to him, "You've got to be kidding me. You really expect me to believe that you say dude man constantly?"

He said, "Yo dude man I don't care what you believe because I say whatever I want, whenever I want, about whatever dude man."

So I'm thinking in the back of my mind that "Dude Man" is laying it on thick because Garret and to a lesser extent Sam wants to prove to me that "Dude Man" is for real. I was game for playing around and so

I talked a little bit to "Dude Man" and he never let down his guard. I thought to myself this guy is good at playing this little role he has for himself. As time wore on and Sigonz showed up and we had to start working "Dude Man" continued to hang around and I pretended I wasn't listening to him but kid you not he said "Dude Man" every damn time he opened his mouth.

It was, dude man this, and dude man that, and no way dude man, or you gotta be kidding me dude man. It was unbelievable. It was so funny. On another level I saw it to be a possible nervous tic. I really think he was saying it without really knowing he was saying it.

I had to tell Garret and Sam that they were right in that, "Dude Man" is a real guy and he is the real thing, he is "Dude Man!"

I swore to myself that I would not allow that phrase into my vernacular but God darn it all to hell because I occasionally found myself saying, dude man. I would say it when someone was particularly driving me mental. I would yell in exasperation, "Dude Man, you don't know what you're talking about."

Long live the Dude Man.

Allen and Matt carried our equipment so much, it's hard to imagine their dedication to our band. They were so much a part of the band I guess like they felt like they were carrying "their" equipment. Keep in mind we were on the Third Floor. For every gig we had we had to un-plug all of our equipment and all of those wires, break down my big drum set which had something like 13 cymbals, heavy cymbal stands, numerous heavy amplifiers, the PA system, monitors, and this huge electrical wire called the snake. Don't forget the multiple guitars, Sam's huge piano and stand, and countless other little things. The average man or woman on the street could not imagine how much work it was for us to break down all of our stuff and then set it back up again in some strange bar somewhere. You have to have a huge burning desire deep within your soul to want to play live music if you're willing to put up with that much turmoil. Third Floor ended up doing exactly 50 gigs in 1989! I could have died and gone to heaven if we had done 20 gigs. I just wanted to get out and play. We played two legendary places on Philly's South Street; J.C. Dobbs and The Bacchanal, which was such a cool place. Miss L. Green showed up at that gig. We also played a place called "Tops" in the city limits. I wanted to be a Rock Star. The drummer from RUSH, Neil Peart, was a huge influence on me. He was always on tour with RUSH. I wanted to get out there and be a drummer on the road too. I would be remiss in my duties if I did not declare that Ginger Baker was a huge influence on me as well. Trying to play the Cream songs accurately was a tremendous challenge. I got Ginger's autograph outside of the Chestnut Cabaret in Philly and it is one of my most precious items.

It was so funny when we were up on the stage at all kinds of gigs people in the audience would shout out "Free Bird." That was so funny. I never got tired of that.

I'm sure that it was the early fall of 1989 when I had told the guys in the band about the movie, "Barfly" and how it was one of my favorite movies. At that time I was not a full-blown movie maniac like I am now-a-days but still, "Barfly" was one of my favorite movies. I couldn't believe that none of those guys had seen it. I had also recently pointed out that we never hung out as a band. We always met up at the studea, ran through all of our songs, had a couple of beers together and then we'd all split because it was after 1 am. We rarely ever just sat around and hung out in a relaxed fashion. I hit those guys with the idea of hanging out in Sam's parents den while watching the Barfly. I was happy when they agreed to just chill out for a while. Of course we drank beer, and got high, and Sam and Phil smoked cigarettes like they were human chimneys. I was very thrilled when I saw all those guys enjoying the movie so much. It really made me happy. I got a real kick seeing Garret and Sigonz laughing hard together during certain scenes or when certain dialogue was spoken. Those guys liked the movie so much that we sat together more than a few times to watch it again. I had so many lines of dialogue memorized that Garret would ask me to say certain lines in the Studea and I could do them with a good Mickey Rourke impersonation and Garret would bust up laughing. The movie became a good source of humor and lightheartedness while the tensions of the band where always there. There is one very important line of dialogue in the movie and that is the line spoken by Wanda when she and Chinaski are walking down the sidewalk at night. The famous line is, "My place is next. I'm up on the Third Floor." All of the guys in the band got a kick out of that. I'm sure that one line of dialogue went a far way in causing those guys to like Barfly so much.

Third Floor was a really great band that played gigs all over the place in Montgomery, Bucks, and Philadelphia counties. The majority of our gigs were in Montgomery County. I thought it was so cool that we got to do a few gigs on Philly's legendary South Street. We had a Halloween party gig in our Third Floor Studea warehouse in October 1988 that was a smashing success. I had never seen so many incredibly professional looking Halloween costumes in my life nor have I to this day. We had a costume competition and it was impossible to pick the best three costumes. We had a second Halloween party at the MSS Hall in Norristown and once again the costumes were off the charts. I don't know what's going on down there in Norristown and Bridgeport but those people know how to get dressed up for Halloween. Many of the costumes looked as if Hollywood specialist had designed them. I'm not messin around. At the 1988 party there was a pregnant Nun, a Mummy wrapped in hospital gauze from head to toe. There were two girls dressed as flappers from the 1920s and that was Daisy and her friend Sherry Doherty. They both looked totally smoking hot sexy. We had a gigantic Gumby. Blaine was dressed in perfect Star Trek garb and his girlfriend Darlene, was dressed as a witch. They made it into the finals. I recently watched that video and was stunned to see that I was the judge. Usually I layed low during things such as this but there I was with the microphone using the crowd applause as the gauge as to who won. A guy dressed as a hooker won. He was really something that night. I could see in the video that Sam played a Roland D-50 and a KORG. After the gig was over I went outside to have a smoke and get some air and I was just in time to see a full blown drunken Gumby walking down the street in the dark. I was laughing under my breath. It was so damn hilarious. Everyone had a mother flipping blast at that party. Back in the day, we had gig after gig. The thing just blew up. We sounded so good and were so professional that we thought we would be discovered. We never got a manager because we could get our own gigs. We settled into a rhythm and became a band that was always on the move. We rehearsed two or three nights a week and usually had a gig or two on some weekends. Month after month went by and this became our life. It was almost too much to believe. I'll never forget the time I walked into Morley's Pub around 7 o'clock and the place was packed with people eating fancy dinners. It was a real nice Irish Pub and loads of our fans were sitting together on a long table and everybody was happy with big smiles on their faces and we were the talent who were going to be playing later that evening on this small makeshift stage.

It was one of those magical moments in my life that I'll never forget. Everyone had such big smiles as they sat in front of their plates filled with fine, delicious food. My heart grew two sizes that night.

As a band we didn't hang out together all that much. We saw so much of each other at rehearsal and gigs that when we had time away from each other we kind of stayed away. I was running through my brain recently and realized that we did go to a few concerts together. There was probably one person missing from each of these concerts and the Sax dude Allen wasn't at any of these shows but almost all of us were there, roadies included. We saw, together, Frank Zappa, REM, Pink Floyd, and The Grateful Dead. That's an impressive line-up. We saw Frank Zappa in the early days of our band. I really wanted to see Frank because he had already been diagnosed with cancer. I knew that seeing him was a very important event. We saw REM when they were at the top of the charts. Garret demanded that Phil and I see the Dead and I was so glad that I did, that we did. What makes this concert list also so cool is where we saw the acts. We saw Zappa at the Tower Theater. REM at the Spectrum. Pink Floyd at Veteran's Stadium and the Greatful Dead at JFK Stadium. How Mother Flippin Cool is that? Only the Tower Theater still stands. All of those other venues are gone! Hard to believe.

There is one story I have to talk about and that is when Garret finally turned 21. It just did not compute that during all of this time Garret was 19 and 20. He had such a confidence that it seemed he was more like our ages of 23 or 25. We had to go to our corner bar, Rossi's, and buy drinks for Garret "legally" for the very first time. Garret had been getting into bars for the past two years because he was "with the band." What a trip. So we go to the bar and I tell the guys I want to do that scene from the Barfly where Henry buys drinks for the whole bar. Here is how the story goes.

We all sat at the bar and there were other people sitting at the bar and in fact the bar was so full there wasn't a seat for Phil or I. I told the bartender to come on over. I said listen buddy my young friend year just turned 21 and you know we're the guys in the band from around the corner. I want to do a scene from the movie the Barfly. I tell the bartender that I'm going to buy everybody at the bar, right now, a shot and I'm going to put it on my credit card. I'm going to say some lines to you that are from the movie that might be a little bit offensive but I just want you to play along. These guys here, my band mates, are probably going to be laughing but don't take offense to it because they know the movie well. I asked the guy okay? He said, okay. So I stood up on the metal bar that runs along the ground and I yelled at everybody "hey everybody sitting at the bar I'm going to buy everybody a shot. A roar of approval rose up. But don't drink it until I make a toast to everybody. I asked everybody, "Do you understand?" They said yes.

So I say to the bar keep in my Henry Chinaski voice, "Hey barkeep give everybody a shot, on me, I'm paying. Why are you still standing there, get trottin boy, my friends are thirsty." Garret busted up laughing on that line. So the bartender has to get out all the shot glasses and go along to each person and ask them what they want and it kind of slowed the action down a little bit. He gets near us and I say something like "come on man, can't you poor those shots any faster. Me my friends need a drink." So he gives me a look already like he's not enjoying this too much. He finishes the last shot and there were probably about 14 barstools in that place. So I put my foot on the foot rail to get myself a little bit up in the air and I raise my shot glass in the air and I turn from left to right from left to right and I shout out things that you would hear Henry Chinaski say. "Hey to all my friends, yeah to all my friends, drink up everybody, to all my friends, yeah"!!! Everybody in the bar is holding their shot glasses in the air and I'm looking from left to right to make sure everybody's included and I looked at some of the faces and they looked so happy holding their shots up in the air. There was a bit of a roar of voices. Most of them probably didn't know who Bukowski was. All they knew was some guy in a bar treated everybody to a shot and they were happy campers for once. I look down at my young guitar player and he has a big smile on his face. I'm pretty sure that he'll never forget that as long as he lives. So everybody threw their shots back and you could hear a bunch of people letting out little moans from the whiskey burning their throats. The bartender came around for my credit card and I wanted to be a big spender just like Henry Chinaski and I didn't want him to remember this as a degrading experience so I purposely threw down a $20 bill in a little bit of a demeaning fashion, as keeping in character, and I said "Hey boy get yourself a shot too, join in on the fun." His eyes got real big when he saw that 20 dollar bill. Then I did it again for just my band mates. We had our selves another toast in the name of the Barfly and in the name of Garret McWillins. We all clinked our shot glasses with all of us saying in our Hank voice, "To all my friends, hey, to all my friends!" This was a wonderful moment and I can tell you that I'm never going to forget it as long as I live.

Another place we the guys of Third Floor hung out was the Rib House in Bridgeport, up the road a mile from our Studea. They had a pool table and a nice size dining room. The food there was really good. The food at Rossi's was just so-so. The two dudes from Sinclair hung out there. I'm talking about the lead singer and the lead guitar player. Those two guys were really good buddies to each other. I'm sure those two had tight telepathy. They were doing some sort of Tuesday night jam night. It was a low pressure jam session. I was there with a few Third Floor groupies, the two roadies, and a few band mates. So, anyway, they started playing some Zeppelin songs. I really wanted to play some Zeppelin because Third Floor didn't play any at all. I very respectfully talked to the singer and asked politely if I could sit in on a few songs and he said no. I was so disappointed. But after some more diplomacy they let me sit in for 2 or 3 Zep songs. I was so happy. I was a little bit drunk too because me and the Third Floor gang had been there eating and drinking and blowing off steam for many hours. Well my beer buzz wasn't enough to throw me off because when the guitar player started and the bass line came in I was on the beat just fine. It's weird how old memories like this come out of the blue sometimes. It's cool for me to be able to say that I jammed with the two main dudes from Sinclair who many years later became the main guys behind "Get the Led Out."

As time wore on and we all started to get tired after about a full year of non-stop gigs and rehearsing we started to lose interest. Maybe I shouldn't say lose interest as I should say we were getting tired of the grind. No one was more tired than me. I had a job doing pharmaceutical research as a senior technician and I was on my feet all day weighing and blending powders, setting up and operating equipment. I was under significant pressure to create innovative ideas. You would have thought I was a PhD with the pressure I had on me. I drummed with a very exacting nature. I tried to play the drum track to each song exactly the same way, over and over again. Neil Peart was my main idol after all. People who saw our live shows would attest to the fact that I played the songs in a very exacting manner. We all played our parts in an exacting manner. We rehearsed on weeknights after I had been at work all day and early on we learned to only accept gigs on Friday and Saturday nights and maybe the occasional Sunday. I was always drinking a lot of beer and not getting much sleep. To quote an old Beru Revue song, "I don't sleep much, I'm never home." I was running deep. I was deep in my cups. Phil worked full time and had a long commute every day. Sam, Sigonz, and Allen were full time students studying music. Sigonz also had a part time job as a waiter. Plus he lived all the way down in the city so every time we had rehearsal or gigs he had to travel all the way up from the city of Philadelphia. Garret had significant stress as he taught guitar lessons all day. Could you imagine teaching guitar lessons all day? I was getting sick of playing the same old songs. We had been playing some of our favorite songs from the early days for 2+ years. We did add and remove songs to keep our set list fresh for our paying fans. The bass player didn't want to say it too loud but he was feeling the same way. I heard him say that, "He was tired of playing the same songs to the same faces in the same places." That is exactly what I was feeling. I wasn't the only one who was tired. I was also having trouble with lateness at work. Imagine drumming your brains out from 10 PM to 2 AM in front of a live audience in a smoke filled bar and then having the audience almost attack you in order to keep you playing. So we would do an encore until 2:10 AM. You run off the stage to a little side room, for instance at the Ambler Cabaret. Your fans and some new audience members are screaming and pounding their feet for more. Everybody wants more. It seemed like Blaine was always there, right up front. There were times that my band mates and I would look at each other, speechless, as people made a dangerous racket and we would think, "Are those people screaming for us?" Some times it didn't seem real, but it was. So you go out to play a blistering song or songs for 10 more minutes until 2:20 a.m. and then you're done. Now you have to wait 30 minutes for people to leave as you drink beer like it is the most important nutrient on Earth. The smokers smoke. I had to bum a smoke from Phil or Sam after each gig to calm my nerves. Every gig I ever did was an absolute assault on my nervous system. Then you have to break down a whole stage FULL of stuff. Heavy Stuff! You then have to carry all of that stuff out to several vehicles of different sizes and shapes. We did have a big old yellow van. That was Sam's vehicle. We called it "The Speak Easy" because it was always stocked with secret beers. That van was critical for us over the years. You're eventually done loading up your shit by about 4:15 AM to 4:30 AM. Now you have to drive home and hopefully you'll be home by 5:15. So now in order to be on time for work you have to get up at 6:30 am. You know that is not going to work so you set the alarm clock for 7:30 and show up at work at 9 AM when you were supposed to be there at 8 AM. Keep in mind you started loading up your equipment at about 5:30 PM the previous day. You drank plenty of beers the previous night, drummed your brains out, carried out more equipment and you're totally exhausted and you have to make pretend your bright eyed and bushy tailed ready to put in a full day of highly productive and inventive work. You can see that this sort of situation can't last forever. Also imagine the intensity of all of the young 20 something rockers across the whole world who do this generation in and generation out in the name of Rock 'n Roll. You can see why I was developing a significant lateness problem at work. If you add up the full year I had put in with Scooter and Phil in "By The Way" and the 2 ¼ years with "Third Floor" that adds up to three years. It is no wonder I was truly exhausted down into my bones. I, myself, the unstoppable human tornado was out of gas. I wanted to quit the band but I told Phil secretly that I couldn't be that guy who calls it quits. I can't be that guy. I can't be the guy who ruins it for the others.

My performance started to slip. There were gigs where I was so tired that I could not mentally keep track of what I was doing let alone finding the energy to be the engine that drove the band. It was about October 1989 and we had gigs booked through December. Our last gig was scheduled at Morley's pub in Norristown for December 9th. We all agreed that we wouldn't book anymore gigs after that one so that we would have time to rest for the holidays. What was really going on for me was that I really *did* want to stop. I think the bass player wanted to stop as well.

We played the gig at Morley's pub and it was always a favorite place for us because they had such fine food there and Guinness on tap. Keep in mind, since we were Rock Stars, that was free Guinness for us. I drummed that show more relaxed than usual and I was trying to take in every moment because I highly suspected that this was going to be our last gig together. I don't think the audience knew anything about us potentially breaking up. The gig went okay as they normally did because we were such perfectionists. When the gig was over we all went upstairs to one of the second floor meeting rooms and the feeling in the air was one of serious tension, exhaustion and the feeling of pending calamity. I was so tired from just drumming another gig that I actually felt physically ill. I felt as if I was coming down with the winter cold that gets in your bones. We sat around. No one was talking. We were all looking at each other waiting for the other person to make a first move. It was a really sad deal. After all of the highs we had been through to now come to this crushing low was too much to take. I'm pretty sure it was Sigonz who was the first to speak up. In so many words he said he was done and that he was sick of the same old thing. As soon as he said that, that cleared the way for me to say that I felt exactly the same way and that I couldn't go on. Then I said the words that I couldn't believe I said but then I said, "I quit." I told everybody I was really sorry but that I had to stop. I told them that I was really physically hurting and couldn't do justice to the songs anymore. Then there was some more silence with people looking at each other with heavy eyes and then Phil, Sam and Garret chimed in with their own feelings and observations. Then there was silence again where we all just sat there looking at each other or looking away. I knew I was never going to have that feeling of being proud to be the drummer in Third Floor. I knew my relationship with those guys was never going to be the same again. In a way there was a real feeling of death in the air. A heaviness hung in the room; fractured and splintered feelings. There was a real feeling as if something, something very special, had just died. The special magic of the early days would never be felt again.

Everybody knew what was going to happen that night because I always spoke to Phil and Phil always spoke to Sam. Sam or Phil contacted Garret then Garret filled in Sigonz. It was how news spread through the band. Everybody knew what was going to happen but we wanted to get through that gig in a professional manner without any problems. It was strange as hell packing up our equipment one last time. I went cold turkey with hanging out with those guys. After having spent every waking moment with them for over two years I didn't want to see any of them. I think they felt the same way. I didn't even hang out with Phil quite a while after the band broke up. Guys who are in band together really get to know each other and love each other very much. No one ever really said I love you guys but the love comes through the musical instrument to each other player. The emotion of each person is expressed through their musical instrument and it forms into the musical expression of each individual song. When the music is right, and the song is right, and the band is right, I assure you there is love energy permeating the air. How many times have you seen musicians on a stage looking at each other and they both have great big smiles on their faces as their playing their tune? That is a smile of love my friend.

I'll tell you what though folks, we had a blast. There are so many stories that could be told. We saw people in the audience do all kinds of crazy things. We saw fights break out, we saw drunks stumbling around, we saw people smiling and hugging each other. The video that Jooles made of us at our 2nd Annual Halloween party at the MSS Hall was fabulous. We really did have people screaming at us at 2 AM for an encore at various gigs. We've heard crowds of 50 people screaming like they were 200 people. We all got to see and hear Garret McWillins do mine blowing guitar solos on so m a n y songs. Phil went from being a good singer who was not very capable in dealing with the audience to becoming a powerful singer who was an excellent front man. Oh, don't forget, he could drum too. Sam's keyboard playing was critical to forming a lot of the individual characteristic of each song by his choice of all sorts of different sounds and textures that were available to him from his fancy keyboard. We used to play "Low Spark of High Heeled Boys" which is a 14-minute song. After about nine months of playing it our way it was now a 25-minute song. That's right, a 25 minute song. We did improvisation all over the place on that song and we blew people's minds again and again. Sam, Garret, and Allen would take turns doing leads while Sigonz provided a backbone but then at times he would go off the reservation and the whole song was being held together by a tiny white thread. I'll never forget the time when we played Low Spark at Morley's Pub and Phil said to me later after the song that, "At one point none of you guys were playing the same song." He was right. At some certain point we hit a place and all of us exploded in different directions. It was what I like to call OOC, "Out Of Control." Garret McWillins and Mitchell Sibbines both ended up writing some seriously good songs. These are songs that 20 years later are still bouncing around inside my head. I listen to the cassettes all the time.

When I was a little boy I had a dream of one day playing in a rock 'n roll band that played music so well that people would go out onto the dance floor and dance a while. My goal was to give people a break from all their worries and cares. I noticed that adults were always in a hurry, that they had 1 million things to do and that there was often yelling and arguing. I knew for sure that adults sometimes needed to go out and have a good time. My dream eventually became a reality when my buddy Phil and I met up with three guys from Norristown. We worked very hard to become good enough to get paying gigs and sure enough we did a lot of gigs. One thing is for sure is that when I laid down the beat and the band joined in; people got up off their chairs and started to dance. We did gig after gig where the whole dance floor was full! The skill of the players of the band I got in was beyond my wildest expectations. Not only could we play fun music but, we could play complicated music for the more discerning fans in the audience. So we could do it all. The little boy grew up to be one happy drumming dude.

CHAPTER NINE
THE THIRD FLOOR MOVIE MYSTERY

Now dear reader it is time to get into the heart of the book. It is time to get into the heart of, "The Third Floor Movie Mystery." What is "The Third Floor Movie Mystery" you ask? Well I will tell you what it is. "The Third Floor Movie Mystery" is the mystery about the phrase "Third Floor" showing up in so many movies. Why is this happening dear reader? I ask you. Why is it happening that the phrase "Third Floor" shows up in so many movies? I am completely perplexed as to why this is happening, has happened, and continues to happen to this day. You might wonder why I care about this and how it was brought to my attention. The reason I care about it should be self explanatory to you by now after having seen that I poured my heart and soul into a band called Third Floor. It was brought to my attention while I was watching movies. After Third Floor broke up I went into a deep funk. It was a deep, deep funk. I focused much of my energies on being on time for work and improving my work performance. On the weekends I enjoyed renting movies from the local Video store. After having been drumming my brains out for essentially over 10 years I really needed to take it easy on the weekends. Every once in a while I would see a movie where they mentioned the phrase Third Floor or I would notice that a scene involved an apartment door that had a 300 number on the door like for instance D308, 316 etc. At one point I wondered was I really seeing that many movies that said "Third Floor" or was I just losing my mind. After a year or so I decided to start writing down a list of the times I heard "Third Floor" mentioned in a movie or saw a 300 series number and for good measure I would write down a scenario whereby the director showed us, from outside a building, that the scene was taking place on the "Third Floor." But, really the *soul* focus was on someone saying the phrase Third Floor. This became a small curiosity for me at first and I was sure that it probably wasn't going to lead to anything but by God it went on year after year. I was flummoxed. I was perplexed. I was flabbergasted. Was this real I asked myself? How could it be that there are so many movies that mention the phrase "Third Floor?" Year after year went by and I had to keep adding new movies to my list. This is now the essence of the book. This is a mystery. This is not a who-done-it type of mystery. This is a mystery where all opinions are valued. This is a mystery where each can conclude for him or herself their own ideas. I, the discoverer of the phenomenon does not have a rock solid answer hence the cause for this to remain a mystery. I do have several ideas, some of which, people will laugh at for sure and I have one or two other ideas that I suspect may be the answer. So sit back in your favorite comfy chair make yourself some salted buttered popcorn and get an icy cold Coca-Cola and settle in for a good mystery.

The first movie on the list of movies that mention the phrase "Third Floor" is Aliens. The second movie is Barfly. Although many people are unaware of this movie to this day and although many people who saw this movie didn't like it or found it revolting it is still a movie that I hold dear in my heart because it captures in many ways the extremely unusual nature of Charles Bukowski.

Technically speaking though I have to place the movie Aliens as first on the list because I had actually seen Aliens prior to Barfly. The rest of this book is going to be set up in a way that shows the chronological order of how this mystery unfolded for me. It is pretty much going to be a long list of movies but I am going to intersperse here and there small stories or comments about the movie listed. This book after all is about movies but I felt it was very important to include all of the back-story so that you could see why I would be so enamored with the phrase Third Floor.

Remember how I said that I had documentation of the phrase Third Floor appearing in many TV shows and I said I wasn't going to share that information. Well I just looked at the list and decided it wouldn't be much trouble to write it down. The reason I'm doing this is because my dear mother just told me at the age of 89 how much she loves the show the Big Bang Theory. She asked me to check it out and of course I did. When I heard them say Third Floor on two episodes *in a row* I figured well what the heck I guess I'll throw on the TV show data that I have. This is not a big list but I wasn't really focusing on TV shows.

Show	Season or Date	What was said
Jay Leno- Tonight Show		When cheers went off the air the cast members said they went and hung out on the Third Floor
Dharma & Greg		
Murphy Brown		Some guy on the Third Floor blew his brains out because cable went out.
Saturday Night Live	10/6/1991	Community College Library skit
Friends	12/14/1995	
Friends	Alec Baldwin Guest	
Deep Space 9		
Love and War (twice)		
Drew Carey		
Herman's Head		
The Norm show		

Seinfeld		Third Floor Hospital
Boston Common		
The Simpsons		
Heroes	Season 3, Disc 2	
Flight of Concords:		Apt. 307
Fringe		Main character Female lead dead boyfriend appears to her from elevator on the Third Floor.
Fringe	Season 2	Cancer guy enters Apt. 304
Spin City		I used to live on the Third Floor with my mother. (So says Richard Kind who I met in a New York City Jewish Deli)
Justified	Long in the Tooth	There is a scene in Room 312
30 Rock		Liz Lemmon's Office is Room 310

The Big Bang Theory	Episode 13 The Bat Jar Conjecture	
	Episode 14 Nerdvana Annihilation	
Revenge	Season 2, Disc 1	Main character Emily Thorne is in a Hospital when heard over the intercom is "Code Blue Room #3 In a later scene she walks beneath a sign that reads "#3 Patients Room 360-378"

For each movie I am going to list the name of the movie, the date that the movie was released, the approximate date that I saw the movie, a brief synopsis of the movie, the major stars who were in the movie, and lastly how the phrase Third Floor appears in the movie or if it is a 300 series room number, that will be explained.

Movie Title: Aliens
Date Released: 7/18/1986
Date Viewed: ~12/18/1986

Major Stars:

Sigourney Weaver	Bill Paxton	Michael Biehn
Carrie Henn	Al Matthews	Jenette Goldstein
Lance Henriksen	William Hope	Mark Rolston
Paul Reiser		

Movie Story:
Ripley's life pod is found by a salvage crew over 50 years after her ordeal. When she is back to full health she finds out that terra-formers are on the exact planet that she had found the alien species. The company had sent a family of colonists out to investigate her story but now all contact is lost with the planet and the colonists. They enlist Ripley and the colonial marines to return and search for the missing people.

Third Floor Quote:
Bill Paxton's character who is a Private and whose name is Hudson is looking for all of the missing humans at the space station that they have arrived at. He says to the others, "Yo, stop your grinnin and drop your linen. Found em." But then

Someone asks, "Are they alive?" Hudson says, "Unknown, but, it looks like all of them, over in the processing station. <u>Sub</u> <u>level 3</u>, under the main cooling towers."

In a later scene when they have made their way over there, Gorman, the pansy of a commander, says to the crew of Marines, "There should be a stairwell. You want <u>sub level 3</u>."

Towards the end of the movie when they lose Newt and Ripley decides to go back to get her she goes down a flight of steps, loaded up with all of her weapons, and right behind her on the wall is a big number <u>3</u>!

You don't need me to tell you how absolutely awesome the Alien movies are or were. The first Alien movie scared the living shit out of me. I saw it when I was a senior in high school and I thought my heart was going to explode. I literally put my hand on my wrist and tried to count my pulse because I was afraid my heart was going to explode. I played Ice Hockey year round, as you know, and I was in tip-top shape but I still feared my heart might explode. That was the first and only time I ever tried to count my pulse in a movie theater. I was really shook-up.

I really like this second movie. I love the character Newt. I love the scene when Private Hudson screams, "Game over man, game over man." That is such a funny scene and yet at the same time, the first time I saw the movie I was scared to death along with that character.

Movie Title: Barfly
Date Released: 9/2/1987
Date Viewed: ~11/16/87

Major Stars:

Mickey Rourke   Frank Stallone
Faye Dunaway   Pruitt Taylor Vince
Alice Krige   Jim Nance
J. C. Quinn

Movie Story:
Henry Chinaski is hard drinking fellow who lives one notch above skid row. Sometimes to ease his despair he'll write some poems. One night in a bar he runs into distressed goddess named Wanda. Those two form a relationship and this movie tells the tale of their drunken madness and entanglements. This movie is a true dark comedy.

Third Floor Quote:
Mickey Rourke and Faye Dunaway's characters meet in a bar. They leave together and stop off at a liquor store to get some liquor, cigarettes, and cigars. They walk to Faye's apartment. Her characters name is Wanda Wilcox and Mickey's characters name is Henry Chinaski. They are walking along a sidewalk at night and Wanda says, "My place is next. I'm up on the <u>Third Floor</u>. Don't worry, there's an elevator"

As they walk along she sees some corn growing up on a small hill. She says, "I love corn." She decides to go up and grab some of the corn but the corn is too young and so it's uneatable. Henry says to Wanda, "Hey wait you can't go up there. That's out in the open. You will be seen. Hey, hey what are you doin?"

Sure enough the cops come by and shine a spotlight on them. They run quickly towards the basement of the building. The cops yell, "Stop Police." Wanda yells quickly to Henry, "Put your finger on that <u>3</u> button."

In a much later scene in the movie we find out that Wanda and Henry live in <u>room 309</u>. We can also see that the crazy guy who beats the crap out of his wife live in a <u>room 308</u>.

There is another scene where Henry and Wanda are outside on a sunny day and they walk in front of the building where they live and the sign says "Royal Palms" and the address is <u>360.</u>

In another scene Wanda says to Henry, "*By the way*, cops came by." Buk says, "Come by where, here." Wanda says, "No, not here, it was next door at <u>308</u>. Two ambulance guys carried him out."

If you recall I grew up in Apt. D-308 in Wissahickon Park Apartments. So what apartment does one of my favorite movie characters of all time get into a fight in? You guessed it; Apt. 308.

If you recall what highway did my Dad drive on 5 days a week, as I did as well? What apartment number did one of my favorite movie characters live in? You guessed it, 309.

Pretty damn spooky kids. Is this just a total coincidence? Yeah, pretty much, but I still get a kick out of it.

There is another spooky coincidence I have just come across. I have just recently bought and watched a DVD called "The Outsiders of New Orleans" (March 2014) which is about John and Louise Webb who were the people who published two books of Charles Bukowki's earliest works. The DVD is fantastic and I recommend it to anyone who is a Bukowski fan. John Webb is long since dead so Gypsy Lou in her 90's provides all of the commentary and the video is a treasure trove of information.

Well something I noticed was that they lived on Royal Street when they made the two legendary Bukowski books of poetry and in the movie "Barfly" Hank and Wanda live in a place called the Royal Palms which obviously has the word *Royal* in it as well.

I just love stumbling upon things such as this. (mad scientist laughter)

As I have mentioned before. I really love this movie. If you recall my Dad was an alcoholic so I have seen first hand a lot of the darkness behind this hideous disease. You might think that I would be then turned off by this movie but I have grown up to learn that you can't hide from the harshness of life. You have to try to cope with the ugly parts of life and so even though this movie has real darkness in it Bukowski is able to somehow bring humor into the movie as well. I was a big drinker in my 20's. I really was. I was living with all of the ugly side effects of that much drinking. Even through it all, all I wanted was another cold beer.

Movie Title: Communion
Date Released: 11/10/1989
Date Viewed: ~4/10/1990

Major Stars:
Christopher Walken
Lindsay Crouse
Frances Sternhagen
Andreas Katsulas

Movie Story:
On December 26th, 1985, Whitley Strieber had a dream. Some time later he discovers his family had the same dream. Months later, he makes a tremendous shocking discovery about his life. You see; he is being visited by Aliens.

300 Series Number:
Towards the beginning of the movie the main character Whitley Strieber burns some Duck in the oven. The firemen come because of smoke. They call in the false alarm. The fireman says into his walkie-talkie, "891 5th St, Apt. 303, he has a 23." You can see the 303 on the door when the firemen leave. Later in the movie when he comes home from a hypnosis session you can see the 303 as plain as day.

In case you don't know what this movie is about, it is about Aliens. Whitley Strieber is a famous Alien abductee. He was abducted many, many times and wrote books about his experiences.

Movie Title: Quick Change
Date Released: 4/27/1990
Date Viewed: ~10/27/1990

Major Stars:
Bill Murray
Geena Davis
Randy Quaid
Jason Robards

Movie Story:
Bill Murray, dressed as a clown, has robbed a New York City bank with the help of two colleagues. But now the real problems begin as all three have to escape from the city.

Third Floor Quote:
Bill Murray is a clown who is robbing a bank by himself. He is on the phone with Jason Robbarbs, who is the Chief of Police. They are talking about how Bill's character is going to sneak out of the bank. Jason say's,"….you switch on a tape recorder, I'm talking to a machine while you crawl out through the <u>Third Floor</u> heating vent."

Movie Title: Navy Seals
Date Released: 7/20/1990
Date Viewed: ~12/20/1990

Major Stars:

Charlie Sheen

Rick Rossovich

Michael Biehn

Joanne Whalley

Movie Story:
A team of Navy SEALs has been called in to rescue an American aircrew that was captured by mid-Eastern terrorists. Lieutenant Curran, who is in charge of the team, discovers that the terrorists have in their possession dangerous high-tech weapons.

Third Floor Quote:
The Seal team is on their mission. They were scopping out the area of their attack and they had Infrared scanning equipment. They could see enemy soldiers. One of the seal team says, "Looks like we've got a slumber party on the <u>Third Floor</u>."

Movie Title: The Two Jakes
Date Released: 8/10/1990
Date Viewed: ~1/10/1991

Major Stars:

Jack Nicholson   Meg Tilly
Harvey Keitel   Madeleine Stowe

Movie Story:
This is the sequel to the legendary movie Chinatown. Private detective
Jake Gittes still carries baggage from the events of the previous film.
He is hired by a gentleman to investigate his wife's potential affair. Mr.
Gittes is once again drawn into a complicated plot involving big oil,
murder, and unbelievably, ghosts from his past.

300 Series Number:
The door to Jack Nicholson's characters office is "Room 310 Gittes
Investigations." In a later scene, at night, he goes into a different office
it is "Private 308." The very last scene is a close-up of the office door
that says "Private 308."

This movie ends with a close up of door with a 308 on it. The director
made a conscience decision to end his movie with a close up of a door
number. What's up with that?

Movie Title: Home Alone
Date Released: 11/9/1990
Date Viewed: ~4/10/1991

Major Stars:

Macauly Culkin	John Heard
Joe Pesci	Catherine O'Hara
Daniel Stern	John Candy

Movie Story:

Eight-year-old Kevin who was accidentally left home alone by his parents and family when they went on vacation seizes the opportunity to have as much fun as possible while he's on his own. Unfortunately for him two moronic burglars have set their sights on Kevin's house. Kevin rises to the challenge with impressive creativity and versatility.

Third Floor Quote:

There is a whole bunch of commotion in the house the night before everybody is going to France. Macauly's character is accused of causing trouble so he is sent upstairs by his mother. She walks him up the steps and they stop in front of a door. The mom says now get upstairs. He says, "I am upstairs dummy." She says, "The <u>Third Floor,</u> go." He says, "It's scary up there."

Yeah man it was scary up there on the real Third Floor. If you didn't learn your drum bits Garret would yell at you. Scary Man.

Movie Title: Rocky 5
Date Released: 11/16/1990
Date Viewed: ~4/16/1991

Major Stars:
Sylvester Stallone
Talia Shire
Burt Young
Tommy Morrison

Movie Story:
Rocky's career is all washed up. A lifetime of fights has him all worn out and if that wasn't enough a lousy crook of an accountant has left him broke. A new young energetic fighter catches Rocky's eye. With fond memories of his own trainer, Rocky decides to help the young fighter as they both seek glory in their own way.

Third Floor Quote:
This is a bit of a stretch on my part but Rocky goes to see his priest at his church and he brings along his new young fighter "Tommy Gun." Rocky yells up to a <u>Third Floor</u> window and the priest comes to the window and gives Rocky and Tommy Gun a blessing.

This is a horrible movie. I would highly advise not watching this movie.

Movie Title: Predator 2
Date Released: 11/20/1990
Date Viewed: ~4/20/1991

Major Stars:
Danny Glover
Gary Busey
Kevin Peter Hall (Predator)
Ruben Blades

Movie Story:
It's 10 years later and the vicious, frightening, invisible Alien from another world is back on earth. The band of mercenaries that first fought with him are painfully aware of his merciless ways. This time the violent creature is drawn to the gang controlled city of Los Angeles. When dead bodies of drug dealers begin to pile up detective Lieut. Mike Harrigan and the police force begin to battle the creature.

Third Floor Quote:
They almost have the Predator trapped in the meat packing plant. Danny Glover's character gets on the headset and tells the head government guy who is in pursuit that the creature has "made" them. He can see their lights. Glover's character tells the top guy, "Ah Kees, he's right behind you. Third Floor structure, right there."

At this point while I'm watching these movies it is just a fun thing I'm doing. I've got a notepad by my comfy chair and when I hear a Third Floor or see an apartment number in the 300's I write it down. Third Floor, the band, was still heavy on my mind, and heart, because I had put so much into it and I was busy listening to all of the cassettes I had of our gigs. I had over 50 tapes.

Movie Title: Backdraft (10)
Date Released: 5/24/1991
Date Viewed: ~10/24/1991

Major Stars:
Robert DeNiro
Kurt Russell
William Baldwin
Donald Sutherland

Movie Story:
This movie centers on two firemen brothers who are always battling each other over the tiniest of infractions. The two have to put their troubles aside because there is a crazy arsonist with a twisted agenda who is setting Chicago ablaze.

Third Floor Quote:
The opening scene is intense because it has a fire on the <u>Third Floor</u> of a building but no one says Third Floor. It is the top floor of the building.

In another scene there is a fire in a high-rise building. The firemen get in the lobby and ask the guard, "Where is it"? The guard says, "I don't know, there are alarms going off from <u>3 </u>different floors."

Movie Title: My Own Private Idaho
Date Released: 10/18/1991
Date Viewed: ~3/18/1992

Major Stars:

River Phoenix	James Russo
Keanu Reeves	William Richert

Movie Story:
Gus Van Sant has produced a masterpiece that has become a cult classic and an icon in gay cinema. This movie focuses on a subculture of people who are often on the grift and trying to make ends meet with small heist.

Third Floor Quote:
One of the several random characters in a diner tell stories of their "tricks" they have to do to get drugs or money. One white kid in a black cap and jacket makes a deal with a black guy who has a lot of Meth and money. The kid was going to give the black guy oral sex. This is what he said. "So the plan was that he was on the <u>Third Floor</u>, so my buddy Scott would hang out on the street. When I got up to the room I was going to toss the money out of the window to Scott."

Movie Title: Prince of Tides
Date Released: 12/25/1991
Date Viewed: ~5/5/1992

Major Stars:

Barbara Streisand   Blythe Danner
Nick Nolte   Kate Nelligan

Movie Story:
A man with heavy emotions has to meet his sister's psychiatrist in New York City after his sister has attempted suicide. As the two people meet on many occasions while discussing his sister and their family history the two begin to fall in love during the process.

Third Floor Quote:
Nick Nolte has a sister who has attempted suicide. She lives in New York City and he travels to see her. Barbara Streisand is her Psychiatrist. They meet in the Hospital the next day. B. Streisand's character is on the phone with somebody when she says, "I have a cancellation so why don't we meet here at the Hospital in 45 minutes, OK? All right, I'm on the <u>Third Floor</u>."

For some reason this movie really got to me when she said Third Floor. It wasn't every day that you heard a movie that said Third Floor in it. I watched a lot of movies that didn't say Third Floor. Sometimes I thought I wasn't going to see any more movies that said it so when Barbara Streisand said this line in this movie I was fired up.

Movie Title: The Public Eye
Date Released: 1/1/1992
Date Viewed: ~6/5/1992

Major Stars:

Joe Pesci   Richard Riehle
Barbara Hershey   Stanley Tucci

Movie Story:

A crime photographer who is the best at what he does gets involved in a conspiracy between rival gangs. This is a period piece that takes place in the 1940's. The photographer has developed ingenious ways to get compelling photos. He does not want to get involved with either side. He just wants the "shots."

Third Floor Quote:

In the opening scene Joe Pesci's character "The Great Bernsenie" is photographing a dead guy with those old-fashioned 1940s style cameras. It is nighttime. There is a small crowd gathered outside in front of the building. The police show up and as they are running up the front steps a woman, who we can assume is the manager, says to the police, "Third Floor" in a subdued way.

Much later in the movie Bersenie is cutting up some black and white photos while sitting at an office desk while a police radio is playing quietly in the background. You have to listen closely but you can hear the voice say, "On the Third Floor, name of Judy Var Haggard, Var Heggert."

This is a real catch on my part to hear the voice say Third Floor in such a quiet way. I didn't notice this the first time I watched the movie.

Later still in the movie where Joe Pesci's character is making calls to find out where the big hit is going to occur and we the viewer can see him in his Third Floor apartment from street level. It is nighttime and a bad guy gangster is watching him.

Movie Title: Toys
Date Released: 12/18/1992
Date Viewed: ~1/18/1993

Major Stars:

Robin Williams

Joan Cusack

Michael Gambon

Robin Wright

Movie Story:
An elderly man dies early in the story and leaves his Toy empire to his fun-loving son Leslie Zevo. Leslie is a guy who hasn't really grown up because he has been playing with toys his own life. Folks wonder if he is up to the task. There is another problem and that is that Leslie has an evil Uncle and he shows up out of nowhere convinced he is going to run the show now. Uncle Leland wants to make war toys and so the battle is set between them.

Third Floor Quote
Robin Williams and his brother inherit a toy manufacturing company from their dead father. They argue as to how to run the company. The older brother is a General and he wants to make better war toys so he hires kids to help him make good war toys. Robin's character confronts his brother about the kids that he thought he saw from an "upper" window. The older brother tries to claim that from a high window the people will appear smaller than they actually are. He says, "If you're looking from the Third Floor window people look very much smaller, that is it."

Movie Title: Citizen Cohn
Date Released: 8/22/1992
Date Viewed: ~1/15/1993

Major Stars:

James Wood	Joe Don Baker
Joseph Bolognana	Ed Flanders
Frederick Forrest	Lee Grant
Pat Hingle	Josef Sommer

Movie Story:

Roy Cohn was a lawyer and a very powerful back room manipulator in Washington DC during the McCarthy era. Now he lays in a private hospital room dying from the complications due to AIDS. As he *lies* there he reflects on his life while ghosts from the past visit him.

Third Floor Quote:

Very early in the first scene after the opening credits they show the hand of a feeble man in a hospital bed reaching for the buzzer. You can hear a woman's voice over the hospital intercom say, "Dr. Sanford please come to the <u>Third Floor</u> family room. Dr. Sanford please come to the <u>Third Floor</u> family room."

Movie Title: Jennifer 8
Date Released: 11/16/1992
Date Viewed: ~4/6/1993

Major Stars:

Andy Garcia	Lance Henriksen
Uma Thurman	Graham Beckel

Movie Story:
A big time cop from Los Angeles moves to a small town and joins the police force. Before he can settle in he is involved in a murder investigation. Using his own ideas that his colleagues don't believe in, he makes progress on the case. During the investigation he meets a young woman by the name of Helena who is blind. Andy Garcia portrays the cop and his characters name is John Berlin. John is attracted to Helena. John is the only cop on the force who believes that they are chasing a serial killer.

Third Floor Quote:
Andy and Uma character's are having a conversation about how cars sound differently. Uma's character is blind. Uma says, "Our kind of car sounds fat. Are you sure you want to see it, it's another three floors up." When Uma and Andy are walking up the steps in a stairwell they walk past a door with the number 351 on it; another 300 series number on a door in a movie.

Later in the movie Andy's character is in the Blind School late at night on Christmas. The school is empty. The creep is in the building. Andy is looking for him. All of a sudden the voice- speaking- elevator says, "You are now on the Third Floor." That means that the creep just used the elevator. Andy goes running after him. Andy gets to the elevator and as soon as he looks up the red number 3 is illuminated.

This movie really got to me. It was kind of spooky. When Andy Garcia's character went into that big school at night when it was snowing and he went snooping around in the dark with just a flashlight and the elevator voice thing said you are on the Third Floor, that really got me. I think this was one of the first movies that made me think, "Okay, what's going on here." How can there be so many movies that say Third Floor in them? What is the deal with this?

Movie Title: Home Alone 2
Date Released: 11/19/1992
Date Viewed: ~4/19/1993

Major Stars:

Macauly Culkin   John Heard
Joe Pesci   Tim Curry
Daniel Stern   Catherine O'Hara

Movie Story:
Here we go again. This time instead of flying to Florida with his family, Kevin ends up alone in New York City. He manages to stay in a fancy hotel with the use of his dad's credit card. He has some problems from a snobby desk clerk and an annoying bellhop. He eventually ends up in an old brownstone where he runs into his two old nemeses and he is determined to spoil their plans to rob an historic toy store.

Third Floor Quote:
Macauly Culkin is in trouble again. His dad says while yelling, "Kevin you walk out of here, you sleep on the <u>Third Floor</u>." Macauly says, "Yeah, so what else is new."

What the hell is going on here? I just saw Jennifer 8 about two weeks ago and we have another Third Floor already? Are you serious?

Movie Title: Mrs. Doubtfire
Date Released: 11/24/1992
Date Viewed: ~4/24/1993

Major Stars:
Robin Williams
Sally Field
Pierce Brosnan

Movie Story:
Robin Williams plays a loving but unpredictable dad named Daniel Hillard. He is estranged from his exhausted spouse and is devastated by a recent court order allowing him only weekly visits with his kids. When Daniel finds out that his ex is looking for a housekeeper he concocts a plan to play the role of his life disguised as an English nanny. He gets the job and gets to spend a lot of time with his children and he becomes their best friend while also being a strong parent figure. He is also a really big hit with his ex wife with out her ever knowing his true identity.

Third Floor Quote:
Robin Williams's character is in his first night of costume as the old British Nanny. He is returning home at night to his place and he runs into his court appointed lady who is supervising his behavior and she wants to see the inside of his apartment. He asks her if she is sure she really wants to walk up all those stairs this late in the day. He says to her, "Are you sure you want to walk in dear? That's three floors, hoofin it all the way."

OK. Now I'm freaked out. Now I'm beginning to think there is some sort of conspiracy going on here. The Third Floors are popping up everywhere.

Movie Title: Passenger 57
Date Released: 11/5/1992
Date Viewed: ~5/15/1993

Major Stars:

Wesley Snipes	Alex Datcher
Tom Sizemore	Bruce Greenwood
Bruce Payne	Elizabeth Hurley

Movie Story:
An infamous terrorists is brilliant at evading capture and has been for a long time. He is also extremely intelligent and horribly ruthless. John Cutter is a famous security expert who doesn't take any crap from anybody. Things get very interesting when the terrorists and several of his henchmen hijack the plane that John Cutter is on.

Third Floor Quote:
In the very beginning of the movie the main bad guy is having plastic surgery on his face. The FBI is already on their way to the hospital. They arrive and the top FBI guys tells the rank and file guys to be very, very careful.

One of the FBI guys says, "Where is he?" The top guy says, "Plastic surgery, Third Floor. He keeps changing his face. If we blow this we won't get another chance.

The bad guys name is "Charles Rain" and he is played by Bruce Payne. He is diabolically tough because he was going to have full facial reconstruction without anesthesia. The FBI crashes into the surgery room and chase him down the hall. He is so diabolically tough that he ran full speed through a glass window from the Third Floor and landed on the ground with some help from an awning.

Seriously?

Movie Title: Loaded Weapon 1 (20)
Date Released: 2/4/1993
Date Viewed: ~7/4/1993

Major Stars:
Emilio Estevez
Samuel L. Jackson
John Lovitz
Whoppi Goldberg

Movie Story:
A prominent LA detective is murdered because she had microfilm, which contained a very interesting recipe. That's right, a recipe. The recipe is for making cocaine cookies. A cop team in the style of "Lethal Weapon" is put together and they try to stop the bad guys before they can dope the whole nation by using the "Wilderness Girls" cookie drive.

Third Floor Quote:
Whoppi Goldberg's character is dying from being shot by the bad guy. She tells the crook to park on Third Avenue. "Hey psst, park on third, you'll never find a spot on Alpine. In a later scene Emelio Estevez and Samuel L. Jackson's characters go up the steps to a possible crime scene. They encounter the two very famous TV motorcycle cops from the show called CHIPS. They are involved in a shootout in a hotel hallway. Samuel shouts, "Is this the Billy York informant shootout"? The black hair cop, Erik Estrada, "Frank" asks the blond hair cop, Larry Wilcox, "Jon". "Is this the Billy York informant shootout?" He says, "ah nah, check out the Third Floor".

It happens again!!! It's really unbelievable. What the Hell is going on here?

Movie Title: The Firm
Date Released: 6/3/1993
Date Viewed: ~11/3/1993

Major Stars:
Tom Cruise
Gene Hackman
Holly Hunter

Movie Story:
Mitch McDeere is a young man who was about to start his life as a lawyer. Prior to taking his bar exam he is approached by a prestigious company called 'The Firm.' They make him a very generous offer, which he accepts. The company showers him and his wife with money and gifts but he is oblivious to the dark side of 'The Firm.' Suddenly two Associates are murdered. The FBI contacts him and they pressure him for answers. All at once his life is ruined. He is given a choice - stay loyal to his company, or work secretly for the FBI. Either way the life he had dreamed of has been shattered. He puts his bright mind to work and realizes there is a way out that puts his priorities at the top.

Third Floor Quote:
Tom Cruise's character sets up an office in the building where he works. He goes on an elevator and pushes 7 while some other guy pushes 9. The elevator stops on <u>3.</u> That's right it stops on 3! Holly Hunter's character gets on. She very carefully switches brief cases with Tom Cruise. The brief cases are on the elevator floor. Ms. Hunter is photocopying the files that Tom Cruise is stealing because those files are going to help Tom win a case against the EVIL firm he works for.

So of course the elevator stops at 3! Out of all the floors in the building, it stops at 3!

Movie Title: A Bronx Tale
Date Released: 9/14/1993
Date Viewed: ~2/15/1994

Major Stars:

Robert DeNiro	Lillo Brancato	Francis Capra
Chazz Palminteri	Kathrine Narducci	Taral Hicks
Joe Pesci	Eddie Montanaro	

Movie Story:
This is the story of Chazz Palminteri's life as he grew up in the Bronx. Robert DeNiro plays the role of his Italian American bus-driving father. Young Francis Capra plays his son Calogero. The top guy in Calogero's neighborhood is a flashy "wiseguy" Sonny played by Chazz Palminteri. Calogero as just a boy, witnesses Sonny commit a murder right on his street and he honors the code of the neighborhood by not telling the cops nothing.

Third Floor Quote:
Chazz Palminteri's character is narrating in the voice of a young boy as himself. He says, "That's my building. I live right there on the <u>Third Floor</u>, 667 East 187 street."

Sure, sure, he lives on the Third Floor. Okay he couldn't make this up. He really did grow up on the Third Floor. But you know what......I get to add it to my list.

Movie Title: Ace Ventura Pet Detective
Date Released: 2/4/1994
Date Viewed: ~7/4/1994

Major Stars:

Jim Carrey   Tone Loc
Courtney Cox   Randall "Tex" Cob
Sean Young
Dan Marino (quick appearance)

Movie Story:
Jim Carrey plays the outrageous role of Ace Ventura - Pet Detective. His assignment is to find the Miami Dolphins missing mascot, a dolphin. He also has to find missing quarterback Dan Marino. He juggles multiple assignments at once and he always gets his man, or beast.

Third Floor Quote:
In the very beginning of the movie Jim Carrey's character delivers a package to a bad guy. The package isn't real. Jim Carrey is there to steal back a precious little dog. We the viewer get to see that the bad guy lives in room 311. On a side note it is intriguing to see that the Miami Dolphins, whom the movie is based around, play the Philadelphia Eagles in a fake Super Bowl and I the writer of this book am an Eagles fan. Ace Ventura gets into a fight with Swoop the Eagles mascot: pretty damn hilarious.

At this point I'm really keeping an eye out during each movie that I watch because it just keeps happening again and again.

Movie Title: Speed
Date Released: 6/9/1994
Date Viewed: ~11/9/1994

Major Stars:

Keanu Reeves   Jeff Daniels
Sandra Bullock   Joe Morton
Dennis Hopper   Alan Ruck
Glenn Plummer

Movie Story:
An extremely disgruntled employee Howard Payne is unhappy with his pension plan and he is out to get major ransom money so he can retire in style. He is a bomb expert and he plans on getting things to go his way. Jack Traven who is a top cop in the LA SWAT division is called in to go up against Mr. Payne. Mr. Payne starts out by rigging an elevator in a high-rise building then he rigs a city bus. The problem is if the bus goes below 55 miles an hour the bomb will explode. There are numerous twists and turns in this extremely intense movie.

Third Floor Quote:
Dennis Hopper plays the bad guy in this movie. He is trying to get ransom money for people he has locked inside of an elevator. He has the elevator rigged with explosives and if he doesn't get his money he will blow up the elevator and the people will fall to their deaths. Keanu Reeves and Jeff Daniels are two cops who show up and ruin his plan. He had to blow up the elevator <u>3 minutes</u> too soon and as a result he lost his <u>3 million</u>.

Keanu Reeves and Jeff Daniels characters realize Dennis Hopper is in one of the freight elevators. They hustle to the freight elevators and by accident end up right inside the elevator with Hopper's character holding a gun to them. Keanu, as "Jack," says to the bad guy, "There's going to be 50 cops waiting for you in the basement." The bad guy says back to him, "Oh, standard flanking deployment right, well maybe we'll get off on the <u>Third Floor.......</u>"

In the next scene the top SWAT guy yells, "I want location on those God damn shots." Another cop says, "Lieutenant, we've got movement on the freight elevator." They all look at the number clicking on a display. It stops on 3 and the Lieutenant says, "It's on 3, let's move!"

Speed was an awesome movie when it came out. Nobody knew who Sandra Bullock was and all the guys loved her instantly. They played this movie over and over again on HBO and I watched it a bunch of times. There are "3's" all over the place.

Movie Title: True Lies
Date Released: 7/14/1994
Date Viewed: ~12/14/1994

Major Stars:

Arnold Schwarzenegger   Tom Arnold
Jamie Lee Curtis   Eliza Dushku
Bill Paxton   Charlton Heston
Tia Carrere   Art Malik
Grant Heslov

Movie Story:
Special agent Harry Tasker is a top spy in the ultra-secret Omega Sector. His wife thinks he is just a very boring computer salesman. When Harry's cover is blown and his wife eventually discovers his true identity the plot becomes even more engaging. Mrs. Tasker is introduced into Harry's world very abruptly and she rises to the occasion. They have to fight international terrorists and they have to fight to save their marriage.

Third Floor Quote:
Arnold's character came to visit Jamie Lee's character at work one day. Jamie Lee had to explain what happened so she said, "..... and so of course, the big problem, our printer shutdown. So I went to the Third Floor to use theirs but they have the 1720......."

Jamie Lee Curtis is smoking hot and she made my day when she said, "Third Floor."

Movie Title: North
Date Released: 7/22/1994
Date Viewed: ~12/22/1994

Major Stars:

Elijah Woods

Jason Alexander

Julia Louis- Dreyfus

Bruce Willis

Abe Vigoda

Dan Aykroyd

Scarlett Johansson

Reba McEntire

Kathy Bates

Movie Story:
11-year-old North is fed up with his parents. They are always too busy with their careers and don't give enough parental attention to him. He decides to file a lawsuit against them. The judge rules that he has two months to find new parents or to return to his current parents. So North travels out on a funny journey around the world to find two parents that will really care about him.

Third Floor Quote:
Elijah Wood's character, North, goes to a mall because his special place is sitting in a leather chair in a furniture store. People leave him alone when he sits there. Bruce Willis walks up and he is dressed up in a pink bunny suit. They start to talk to each other.

Bruce: So, who are you?

North: I'm North.

Bruce: I see your name on maps, very impressive.

North: Who are you?

Bruce: I am the Easter Bunny. <u>Third Floor</u>, Toys.

Movie Title: While You Were Sleeping
Date Released: 6/27/1995
Date Viewed: ~11/27/1995

Major Stars:

Sandra Bullock

Bill Pullman

Peter Boyle

Jack Warden

Monica Keena

Micole Mercurio

Movie Story:

Here is a love story built on a misunderstanding. A female transit worker pulls commuter, Peter, off of the tracks after he's been mugged. She saved his life. She has a crush on him and visits him in the hospital while he is in a coma. His family members mistakenly assume that she is Peter's fiancée and in the rush of confusion she doesn't correct them. Things get even more complicated when Peter's brother and her start to fall for each other. He is somewhat suspicious of her and eventually all of the truths must reveal themselves.

Third Floor Quote:

Towards the end of the movie Sandra Bullock's character Lucy is in her apartment. Her male neighbor Joe Jr. who really has the hots for Lucy is in the hallway with a cute looking blonde haired woman. The non-coma brother Jack has come to Lucy's building and he runs into Joe Jr. in the hallway.

Joe Jr. says to Jack, "Hey, are you going to see Lucy? She is the best lookin chic in this building." The blonde woman says, "Hey"! She is offended.

Joe Jr. responds by saying, "But you are the best lookin chic on the Third Floor." The blonde chic's name is Phyllis.

Very close to the end of the movie Joe Jr. comes by to visit Lucy after she confessed to everything at her wedding to the coma brother. Joe Jr. wanted to see if Lucy was all right.

Then Lucy asked Joe, "So umm, how are things going with Miss <u>Third Floor</u>." Joe Jr. starts to cry.

Okay folks now I'm beginning to think there **is** some sort of Third Floor conspiracy. But, what is the conspiracy?

Movie Title: Apollo 13
Date Released: 6/30/1995
Date Viewed: ~11/30/1995

Major Stars:

Tom Hanks	Ed Harris
Bill Paxton	Kathleen Quinlan
Kevin Bacon	Gary Sinise

Movie Story:
Technical troubles scuttle the Apollo 13 lunar mission in 1971, risking the lives of astronaut Jim Lovell and his crew. Ron Howard did an amazing job directing the occurrences of this true-life story. All of the men on board this small spacecraft surely would have died if it wasn't for the old American "Can Do" philosophy. It is astonishing to think that they drifted 200,000 miles from earth. The astronauts and the ground crew worked in ingenious ways to avert tragedy.

Third Floor Quote:
Tom Hanks's character runs into some reporters in a warehouse where scientist were assembling rocket parts. A voice comes over the loudspeaker and says, "Attention all personnel, clear <u>level 3, level 3</u>."

So, umm, why did they have to clear Level 3?

Is it safe to say that Tom Hanks is one of my top 10 favorite actors of all time? YES!

Movie Title: High School High
Date Released: 10/25/1996
Date Viewed: ~3/25/1996

Major Stars:

John Lovitz	Louise Fletcher
Tia Carrere	Mekhi Phifer

Movie Story:
No one knows why for sure why Richard Clark decided to leave the well-known Wellington Academy to teach at Marion Barry high school. Now that he is there he is going to try to motivate the D average students into making good grades as well as to try to woo a fellow teacher.

Third Floor Quote:
Jon Lovitz is in the teachers' lounge. He walks over and introduces himself to a black guy who is sitting on a couch reading Soldier of Fortune magazine.

Jon says, "Hi I'm Richard Clark. I'm the, ah history teacher here. The black guy says, "umm huh."

Jon says, "What department do you teach in?"
The black guy says, "I don't know, something up on the <u>Third Floor</u>."

Special note: something is really mysterious here. The theme song of the Jeopardy game show is quietly playing in the background while this scene is occurring. This is really spooky because we all know that Third Floor played this song and we called it Jeopardy Funk.

This blows my mind and this is the first time that I think that maybe the people in Hollywood know about my band "Third Floor" but how in God's name is that possible?

(I'm kidding. Relax.)

Movie Title: Nick of Time (30)
Date Released: 11/22/1995
Date Viewed: ~4/22/1996

Major Stars:
Johnny Depp
Courtney Chase
Christopher Walken
Charles S. Dutton

Movie Story:
An ordinary man named Gene Watson gets off a train at Union Station in Los Angeles along with his six-year-old daughter Lynn. Gene is a public accountant. Two sinister people who have a frightening plan that they are about to put into motion approach Gene and grab him and his daughter. He is informed as to what he has to do if he ever plans on seeing his daughter alive. They intend him to commit murder that very afternoon.

Third Floor Quote:
Johnny Depp's character asks a guy who is a bellhop, "Excuse me, can you tell me where the Emerald Bay room is?"

The Hispanic bellhop guy answers back, "It's the Third Floor, yellow stairwell, follow the signs."

On the Third Floor Johnny walks abruptly into a guy and at that exact moment there is a big yellow number 3 behind them on the wall. A second or so later they do a close-up on Christopher Walken and the number 3 is right behind him. Later when Johnny Depp's character goes to the men's room he walks by the big number 3.

OK this is too much. Here is another movie where everybody is talking about the Third Floor and big #3's are featured in the background. What the hell is going on? My fun little game of documenting the prevalence of Third Floors in movies is starting to freak me out a little bit.

Movie Title: Heat
Date Released: 12/14/1995
Date Viewed: ~5/14/1996

Major Stars:

Al Pacino	Tom Sizemore	Natalie Portman
Robert DeNiro	Diane Venora	
Val Kilmer	Hank Azaria	
Ashley Judd	Amy Brennerman	

Movie Story:
Tremendously intense thief McCauley leads a top-notch crew on various military style robberies around the LA area. An equally obsessive detective by the name Hanna tracks after him. Each man is aware of the other and is respectful of the others dedication and knowledge. However there is no illusion on either man's part as to their willingness to kill each other if the opportunity were to present itself.

Third Floor Quote:
Towards the end of the movie, DeNiro as a bad guy, is driving off into the sunset with his woman. He gets a call in his car and finds out that one of the guys from his crew who killed two security guards in the beginning of the movie is staying at a local hotel. Even though DeNiro could have driven off into a life of peace he drives to the hotel with the intense urge to kill the dirty creep who botched their big heist. DeNiro manages to put on a hotel uniform so that he blends in with the staff. As he is walking past two Hispanic women in a laundry room the one woman says something to the other woman that I can't quite figure out but, then you very clearly hear her say,".........<u>Third Floor</u>, you should have seen".......*unintelligible*. DeNiro finds what room the bad guy is staying at and he says to him through the door, "Security, there is a fire on <u>3</u>, we have to evacuate all floors."

I must add the scene in the end when Val Kilmer is trying to go see Ashley Judd to see if he can grab her so they can escape. The cops have her place surrounded and he is questioned in his car by a cop when he

122

gets close to her place. The cop says over his walkie-talkie, "This guy is John Peterson, valid ID. Car is registered to the last name <u>Bukowski</u>, first name Gene." The cops let Val Kilmer go even though he was the bad guy they were looking for.

I was stunned to hear the name Bukowski since I loved the Barfly so much and by this point I had read 13 or 14 of his books. I have been reading them slowly so that I always have something to look forward to.

Movie Title: Father of the Bride II
Date Released: 12/8/1995
Date Viewed: ~5/16/1996

Major Stars:

Steve Martin
Diane Keaton
Martin Short
B.D. Wong

George Newbern
Kimberly Williams-Paisley
Kieran Culkin

Movie Story:
George Banks has barely had time to recover from his daughter's wedding when he finds out that she is pregnant. That news is not so hard to accept but when he finds out his own wife Nina is expecting too that's when things get a little hard to handle. Him and his wife had been thinking about selling their big home but that's a plan that is gonna have to change now that there is soon going to be the arrival of both a child and a grandchild at the same time.

Third Floor Quote:
From inside an elevator we look up to see the <u>number 3</u> and then the door pops open on the <u>Third Floor</u>. Then the characters walk in a doctor's office with a very good look at the room number, which is <u>306</u>.

New scene: They are leaving the doctor's office and Steve Martin and Diane Keaton's characters are getting in the elevator and out walks Martin Short's character Fronk, and you can see the <u>number 3</u> on the wall of the elevator entrance.

This happened a few days after I just saw Heat. I am stunned. It really has me wondering. What is going on here? What is the deal with Third Floor and 300 series apartment appearing in movies all the time?

Does someone out there know the answer?

Movie Title: Spy Hard
Date Released: 5/24/1996
Date Viewed: ~10/24/1996

Major Stars:

Leslie Nielsen

Nicollette Sheridan

Charles Durning

Marcia Gay Harden

Barry Bostwick

Andy Griffith

Movie Story:

General Rancor is a mad man and he has a missile at his secret base and he is threatening to destroy the world. However in order to launch his missile he needs a special computer chip invented by the brilliant scientist Professor Ukrinsky. Since this is a matter of global significance special agent Dick Steele is assigned to the case in order to prevent potential calamity.

300 Series Number:

Leslie Nielsen's character walks into a hotel room but the door is open already. He slowly walks past the door. You can see the <u>number 304</u>.

Movie Title: Chain Reaction
Date Released: 8/2/1996
Date Viewed: ~1/2/1997

Major Stars:

Morgan Freeman   Fred Ward
Keanu Reeves   Kevin Dunn
Rachael Weiss   Brian Cox

Movie Story:
Two brilliant researchers working on a revolutionary green alternative energy project are chased when they are framed for murder and treason.

Third Floor Quote:
Keanu Reeves's character, Eddie, gives a walk home to Rachel Weisz's character Lily because they are both a bit drunk because they celebrated the successful experiment to prove their "free energy" production program. They are outside a nice big house on a cold night with snow covering the ground.

Lily says, "Here we are."

Keanu says, "This is Allister's house?"

Lily replies, "Isn't he sweet? He lets me live on the <u>Third Floor</u>."
She says this line with a very cool, breezy British accent

Movie Title: Maximum Risk
Date Released: 9/13/1996
Date Viewed: ~2/13/1997

Major Stars:

Jean-Claude Van Damme   Natasha Henstridge
Zach Grenier   Paul Ben-Victor

Movie Story:

A French policeman travels from France to New York City and takes the place of his twin brother. His brother had been killed and he figures he can act as if he is his brother to potentially catch his brother's murderers. He inherits his brother's problems and his beautiful girlfriend. He has to tangle with the FBI and the Russian mafia. Answers are hard to come but he is determined to prevail.

300 Series Number:

Jean Claude's character, Alain goes to New York City to see where and how his long lost twin brother lived. He goes to a Russian club where a skinny white woman pulls him aside. She was his brother's girlfriend and she kisses him aggressively. She doesn't know that he isn't who he appears to be. She hands him a key. The number on that key is 323.

Jean Claude's character goes to the flea bag hotel where the woman Alex lives and he says to the hotel clerk, "Hi, the last time I was here I stayed in ahh room 323, kind of good luck thing. It's available?" The clerk responds, "Nope, but I got 305 across the hall."

A little while later, Alex, who is played by Natasha Henstridge, comes home to the hotel. Jean Claude opens his door and tells her to stay with him. In no time the Russian bad guys show up and break down the door to 323. Since Alex isn't there they go down to the desk clerk and yell at him.

The clerk says, "Look I'm positive the girl went up to <u>323</u>. The top-dog Russian guy shows a picture to the clerk of Alain's brother Mikhail and asks him, "Do you recognize this man?" The clerk says, "Yeah, yeah, he, he checked in across the hal<u>l, room 305</u>. The Russian guy says, "<u>Room 305</u>, OK, good, let's go" to his colleagues.

Movie Title: Godzilla
Date Released: 5/19/1998
Date Viewed: ~10/19/1998

Major Stars:

Matthew Broderick	Harry Shearer
Hank Azaria	Vicki Lewis
Maria Pitillo	Jean Reno
Kevin Dunn	Michael Lerner

Movie Story:
A freighter is violently attacked in the Pacific ocean. A team of experts is called in. The experts include biologists Niko Tatopoulos and scientists Elsie Chapman and Mendel Craven. They conclude that a gigantic reptile is the culprit. Before you know it the massive lizard is on the loose in Manhattan destroying everything in its path. The team and authorities chase the monster to Madison Square Garden where a showdown ensues.

Third Floor Quote:
Matthew Broderick's character is being chased by a baby Godzilla. He jumps into an elevator right before being attacked / eaten. As soon as he jumps in, the elevator goes up and he looks up to see the red <u>number 3</u> (AGAIN!) [alah -- Jennifer 8]. But then the door automatically opens and there are big Godzillas eating a huge bowl of popcorn. Matthew sarcastically says, "Wrong Floor", as several Godzillas look at him curiously.

Seriously Dudes...... what the F is going on here?

Movie Title: La Cucaracha
Date Released: 4/23/1999
Date Viewed: ~9/23/1999

Major Stars:
Eric Roberts
Joaquim de Almeida
Victor Rivers
James McManus
Tara Crespo

Movie Story:
A desperate American writer ends up in Mexico where he is drinking his days away in a tragic manner. He has fled some ugliness in his life back in the states. He is made an offer by the Mexican mob to murder a horrible man. His payment will be generous. However he is doublecrossed but manages to survive.

Third Floor Quote:
Eric Robert's character, Walter, wants to get a room on the Third Floor even though he is crippled. He is in a wheelchair because he was double-crossed and shot in the back. He wants to be up high in his room so he can look out and around. He is trying to explain himself but he is in Mexico and the woman clerk speaks Spanish.

He says, "Tres por favor. No. Yes senorita I want the <u>Third Floor</u>." He ignores her and he drags himself with his arms only up the steps to the <u>Third Floor</u>.

Movie Title: House sitter
Date Released: 6/12/1999
Date Viewed: ~11/12/1999

Major Stars:

Steve Martin

Goldie Hawn

Dana Delany

Suzanne Whang

Donald Moffat

Peter Mao Nicol

Movie Story:

Architect Newton Davis builds his dream house then proposes marriage to his girlfriend only to be rejected. He finds comfort in a one night stand with a waitress who has an uncontrollable imagination. She immediately poses as his wife and with her nonstop verbal delivery has the whole town convinced in no time. It is as if the whole town feels like they know him even though they never met him.

Third Floor Quote:

Steve Martin goes up to see the boss. He says, "I um my name is Davis, I'm an architect on the <u>Third Floor</u>. Do you think Mr. Moseby might have a second, some time to see me?" The secretary says, "Uhh, Let me check. Mr. Davis from the <u>Third Floor</u> to see you. OK, go right on in."

Again and again with the Third Floor. Now my main man Steve Martin is saying it now.

Movie Title: Blue Streak
Date Released: 9/17/1999
Date Viewed: ~2/17/2000

Major Stars:
Martin Lawrence
Luke Wilson
Dave Chappelle
Peter Greene

Movie Story:
Miles Logan is a jewel thief who stole a big diamond but on the night of the theft he had to hide the diamond in a ventilation shaft in a building that was under construction. He only had to serve two years in jail because when the cops cornered him he was empty-handed. Upon his release he goes back to the location only to find that the building is a police building. He has to pose as a police officer in order to gain access to his stashed away diamond.

Third Floor Quote:
Martin Lawrence's character has just stolen a huge diamond. The cops show up on the scene and his escape plan to make it on to the roof of a different building is compromised. He makes it into the other building, which is under construction but the cops are hot on his trail. He has to hide the diamond somewhere so he thinks fast and he places the diamond in a heating air-conditioning vent. He has to memorize the location of the vent because he knows he is going to prison for a long time. The vent location was AC Vent <u>3rd Floor</u> NORTH WING.

Martin Lawrence's character gets out of prison and goes back to the building where he left his big blue diamond and it is a police department building. He is flabbergasted. He reads the directory in the lobby and it says, '<u>3rd Floor</u>: ROBBERY HOMICIDE."

In another scene he is back in the police building and he has to get into an elevator crowded with cops. He pauses and one of the cops asks if he is going up. And he says, "Yeah, Yeah, Ah, Ah, <u>Third Floor</u>."

At this point I am really wondering what is going on. I am beginning to think about this while I am at work. My note pad is filling up and I am going to have to get another note pad. What the bleep is going on? Who ever heard of such a thing? I haven't told anybody about this. I'm still just keeping track while I watch movies because it is something fun to do.

Movie Title: The Million Dollar Hotel   (40)
Date Released: 2/2/2001
Date Viewed: ~7/2/2001

Major Stars:
Mel Gibson
Milla Jovovich
Jeremy Davies

Movie Story:
Someone dies at the Million Dollar Hotel but did they jump or were they pushed. There is a bunch of strange people living at this hotel and many of their stories intertwine. The film was made in collaboration with Bono and the soundtrack is also from U2.

There isn't a Third Floor quote in this movie but as listed above the movie ends with a song by U2 and the chorus of the song is the name of one of Charles Bukowski's Books. I am listing this here because it is as good a place as anywhere else. It is in the order of movies as I had seen them. The name of the Bukowski book is, "The Days Run Away Like Wild Horses."

Bono is a big fan of Charles Bukowski. I think it is safe to say that Bono read all of Buk's work. Mr. Bukowski was actually invited to a U2 concert out in California. He went to the show with his wife. Bukowski's influence is much wider then the average person is aware.

Movie Title: Enemy at the Gate
Date Released: 3/16/2001
Date Viewed: ~8/1/2001

Major Stars:

Jude Law   Joseph Fiennes
Ed Harris   Bob Hoskins
Rachel Weisz   Ron Perlman

Movie Story:
Jean-Jacques Annaud is responsible for this masterpiece that was made in 2001. The movie focuses on an expert sniper in the Russian army and how the Germans had to figure out a way to neutralize this sniper. The story occurs during World War II and focuses on the battle for Stalingrad.

Third Floor Quote:
One of our Russian snipers sends for the Jude Law character. When Jude gets there the sniper says to Jude, "Look, <u>Third Floor</u>, 4th window from the left."

If you have not seen this movie you have to rent this movie right away. This is a fantastic movie. When I see a movie like this, of this quality, I am enthralled. I would love to meet the director over dinner and some drinks and just listen to the man talk. The sets that were created for this movie are beyond perfection. I felt like I was at war on Russian soil in the 1940s. I watched this movie again and again when it came on HBO. You owe it to yourself to watch this movie.

Movie Title: 3000 Miles to Graceland
Date Released: 2/23/2001
Date Viewed: ~7/31/2001

Major Stars:
Kurt Russel
Kevin Costner
Courtney Cox
Christian Slater

Movie Story:
The plan for the robbers was as good a plan as any. They planned on hitting the Riviera casino's count room during an Elvis impersonator convention. But one of the men, Thomas Murphy, decided to keep all of the loot for himself and shot all of the other guys. He even shot recently freed ex-con Michael Zane. With 3.2 million on the line and with the law closing in Michael must get to Murphy first.

Third Floor Quote:
A group of guys are going to rob a casino. They are all dressed like Elvis. Kurt Russel's character is in an elevator and has wires hooked up to the controls of the elevator. Security personnel push the button on his elevator and it starts descending to them on the first floor. Kurt is able to stop the elevator by cutting the red wire and it stops on the <u>Third Floor</u>. You can plainly see the red LED <u>#3</u>. By doing this he is able to avert being caught.

I was so happy when the elevator stopped on number three because now it is at the point while I'm watching movies that if there is ever an elevator involved I'm rooting out loud for it to stop on level 3 or the Third Floor.

Movie Title: Harry Potter and the Philosopher's Stone
Date Released: 11/14/2001
Date Viewed: ~5/1/2002

Major Stars:

Daniel Radecliff	Maggie Smith	Alan Rickman
Emma Watson	Robbie Coltrane	Richard Harris
Rupert Grint	Ian Hart	Verne Troyer
Tom Felton		

Movie Story:
Harry Potter has lived under the stairs at his aunt and uncle's house his whole life. However on his 11th birthday things are going to change. He learns he is a powerful wizard. Not only that but a place has been reserved for him at the Hogwarts School of Witchcraft and Wizardry. He learns to develop his newly found powers with the help of the school's wonderful headmaster. As time goes by, Harry uncovers the real story behind his parents death and about the villain responsible.

Third Floor Quote:
Prof. Dumbledore says, "Also our caretaker Mr. Filtch has asked me to remind you that the Third Floor corridor on the right-hand side is out of bounds to everyone who does not wish to die a most painful death, thank you."

Harry, Hermione, and Ron are on a stairwell that moves on them and dumps them in front of a door. They go through the door and Ron says, "Does any body feel like we shouldn't be here?" Hermione says, "We're not supposed to be here. This is the Third Floor. It's forbidden!" Harry says, "Let's go."

Later still in the movie Hermione finds out about Nicolas Flamel. He is the only known maker of the Sorcerer's Stone. Hermione says, "That's what Fluffy's guarding on the Third Floor. That's what's under the trap door; the Sorcerer's Stone."

Towards the very end of the movie Harry finds out that it is Professor Quirrell who is behind the dastardly deeds of late. Prof. Quirrell knew no one would expect him of being a bad guy. It was he who was trying to get to the Sorcerer's Stone. He says to Harry, "When everyone else was running about the dungeon he went to the <u>Third Floor</u> to head me off." He is speaking of Prof. Snape.

Oh My God Folks!!! Four Third Floor quotes in one movie. I am thankful to the Gods. It would seem unlikely that J.K. Rowling was a fan of Third Floor considering the fact that she lived in England and as far as I remember we never did a tour of England although I was often very drunk back in those days. So I guess we'll have to chalk this up to being a total coincidence.

Although, I don't know the true origins of the Third Floor Movie Mystery. Perhaps it is much deeper and goes back much further than anyone of us could imagine.

Movie Title: Resident Evil
Date Released: 3/15/2002
Date Viewed: ~ 8/15/2002

Major Stars:

Milla Jovovich

Eric Mabius

Michelle Rodriguez

James Purefox

Martin Crewes

Colin Salmon

Movie Story:

A deadly virus escapes from a top-secret facility. It is believed that the virus broke free by accident but did it? The virus turns all of the researchers into ravenous zombies and their lab animals into mutated monsters from hell. The government sends in a fast acting task force to contain the outbreak. Alice and Rain are in charge of the mission. They only have three hours to prevent global outbreak.

Third Floor Quote:

In the beginning of the movie a sinister looking vile which probably contains a nasty virus is broken inside a laboratory in a building full of people working. Some people, in the mad rush to get out of the building, are caught in an elevator. Suddenly they hear an elevator going pass them and they can hear peoples' screaming voices. That elevator crashes into the ground and of course everyone is killed. Suddenly their elevator begins crashing to the ground then all at once it stops, on <u>floor number 3</u>. We look up to see the red LED lights of a number 3.

Why did the writer of this script have the elevator stop on floor #3? Why didn't the elevator stop on floor #4 or perhaps floor #6? This is the question at the heart of the "Third Floor Movie Mystery."

Movie Title: Panic Room
Date Released: 3/29/2002
Date Viewed: ~9/1/2002

Major Stars:
Jodie Foster
Kristen Stewart
Forest Whitaker

Movie Story:
A divorcee and her daughter are in their home, which is a brownstone in New York City when three burglars enter. The mother and daughter manage to make it into their aptly named panic room. The burglars know they are there and a tense and horrible game develops. The intruders are trying to their wits end to break into the panic room.

Third Floor Quote:
Jodie Foster is being shown an incredible brownstone in New York City. A male real estate guy is showing her around. He eventually says, "<u>Third Floor</u>, spare bedrooms, den, what have you. Mr. Perlstein used this as an office."

New Scene: The bad guys are in the house and Forester Whitaker's character says to the other bad guys, "There's a little girl on the top floor, there is a woman on the <u>third</u>."

Movie Title: Sam I Am
Date Released: 12/28/2001
Date Viewed: ~10/1/2001

Major Stars:
Sean Penn
Michelle Pfeiffer
Dakota Fanning

Movie Story:
Sam has the mental capacity of a 7-year-old. He has a daughter with a homeless woman. As soon as the baby is born the woman runs out of the hospital. Sam has to raise the child he names Lucy on his own. But as Lucy grows up Sam's emotional limitations begin to be more of a problem. Authorities have no choice but to take her away. Sam gradually wins over high priced lawyer Rita into taking on his case for free and in turn helps her with the limitations she had been having with her own family.

Third Floor Quote:
Sean Penn is the main character and he is going up an elevator and he says he has to get off at the Third Floor in a Hospital where girlfriend is giving birth. He says, "I have to go to <u>room 324</u> on the <u>Third Floor</u>."

Later in the movie Michelle Phiefer's character and Sam walk up flights of outdoor steps that are part of a parking garage and they walk past a very large painted number <u>3 </u>on the wall.

So now that this has been going on for over 10 years I got to the point where I proposed an idea to myself that I'm sure will be laughed at by serious minded folks. But please keep in mind that this is not some sort of deadly serious book rather it is a lighthearted book meant for fun. I have begun to think that there could be an underground Third Floor band base that traverses from the East Coast all the way to the West Coast. You say, "Dan, you must be kidding us?" I say, "Please play along."

What you don't know is that our legendary guitar player Garret McWillins was a huge Grateful Dead head. He had numerous friends that would come to our early gigs in our super cool Third Floor studea and they would shout out Grateful Dead songs they wanted us to play. The only Grateful Dead song we ever really played was "Gimme Some Love" which wasn't written by the Grateful Dead. I remember someone shouting out, "Play Mama Tried." I have no idea what song that was because I wasn't an intense Dead Head. It looks like Garret decided in the early goings of our band not to be a Grateful Dead tribute band.

Everybody knows that Deadheads record and share bootleg tapes with all the other Deadheads. Garret participated in this activity. Since I was recording all of our parties that we had in our Studea there was a growing collection of tapes. I am sure that the Bridgeport and Norristown people were sharing tapes amongst themselves. Is it possible that cassette tapes of Third Floor made their way across this great country? Possibly. Who's to say?

Movie Title: Pluto Nash
Date Released: 8/15/2002
Date Viewed: ~?2/1/2003

Major Stars:

Eddie Murphy   Joe Pantoliano
Randy Quaid   Rosario Dawson

Movie Story:

It is the year 2087. This story takes place on the moon. Eddie Murphy stars as Pluto Nash. He is the super successful owner of the hottest club in town, or actually the universe. Pluto is pressured to sell his club to gangster types and when he refuses they make life difficult for him, very difficult.

A Number 3 Scenario:

Eddie Murphy's character, Pluto Nash, has to get a hotel room because his Club got blown up. The hotel clerk gives him room <u>3D</u>. A little later the bad guys come around looking for Eddie and his two companions and you can see <u>3D</u> on the door for a brief second.

This is a horrible movie. Do not watch this movie. If you watch this movie you will realize that you just wasted an hour and a half of your life. Don't do it. Eddie Murphy has made very many good movies. I love "Trading Places" for instance. Everybody has a flop now and then. Eddie Murphy was legendary on Saturday Night Live. I still sometimes mumble to myself, "Kill My Landlord." I have seen every episode of Saturday Night Live. I love that show tremendously. I would donate my left gonad to science in order to get in to see just one show. I don't know what science would do with my gonad but, I'm willing.

Eddie Murphy was great along with Nick Nolte in the cop movies "48 Hours." Eddie Murphy was also really good in the "The Nutty Professor."

Keel My Lanlor.

Movie Title: Amelie
Date Released: 2001
Date Viewed: ~2/15/2003

Major Stars:
Audrey Tautou, Mathieu Kassovitz, Rufus, Lorella Cravotta, Serge Merlin, Jamel Debbouze, Clotilde Mollet, Claire Maurier, Isabelle Nanty, Dominique Pinon

Movie Story:
This is a wonderful movie that stars impish Amélie. She is the central character woven through several enjoyable stories. One of the stories involves her finding a small box of little boy toys that had been hidden behind a baseboard tile in her bathroom. She is driven to find the owner of this long lost treasure.

Third Floor Quote:
Amelie is searching for a grown man who as a young boy would have hidden a box of his toys behind a tile on the floorboard of a bathroom where Amelie now lives. She is searching for people who have the last name Bredoteau. She goes to the 2nd person on her list and she speaks into an intercom microphone to the person and they say, "Come up, Third Floor."

This is a French movie for those of you who have no clue. You have to see this movie. This is a wonderful, wonderful movie. This movie is so great that I purchased it on DVD so that I could mail it to my mom and my sister who live in California. They both loved it. I truly believe that any person who watches this movie will love it. I must express to you in no uncertain terms that you must watch this movie. It will cause you to experience joy. All you have to do is look at Amelie's face and you will smile.

Movie Title: Being There
Date Released: 12/19/1979
Date Viewed: ~3/1/2004

Major Stars:

Shirley MacLaine   Melvyn Douglas
Peter Sellers   Jack Warden

Movie Story:
A very simple minded man named Chance has been a gardener for an old man who lived in the Washington DC area. When the elderly man dies Chance is put out on the street with absolutely no knowledge of how the real world works except for what he has learned from watching television all his life.

Third Floor Quote:
Peter Sellers's character, Chance, gets his leg hurt by Shirley MacLaine's character's Limo driver by getting his leg lightly crushed between car bumpers. They take Chance back to Shirley's husband's mansion. Shirley says, "Wilson, would you take Mr. Gardner to the <u>Third Floor</u> guest suite."

***Special note:** This movie is out of chronological order. This movie was made in 1979, which, is well before the Third Floor rock phenomenon occurred. It is also before the movie Barfly occurred. Therefore it does not apply to either of my theories. But wait you say, I don't have a Barfly theory, but soon I will tell you about it.

I have to make a random shout out to a movie called "Adventures of Power." If you like music, drumming, and laughing then you have to rent or own this movie. This movie is Crazy Hilarious, to coin a phrase. I own this movie because my Grand Hero Neil Peart makes a cameo appearance at the end.

Movie Title: Harry Potter: The Prisoner of Azkaban   (50)
Date Released: 5/31/2004 (UK)
Date Viewed: ~11/1/2004

Major Stars:

Daniel Radecliff	Gary Oldman	Michael Gambon
Emma Thompson	Emma Watson	David Thewlis
Robbie Coltrane	Maggie Smith	Rupert Grint
Alan Rickman	Tom Felton	

Movie Story:

Harry, Ron and Hermione return to Hogwarts Academy for their third magic filled year in this follow up movie to the first two Harry Potter blockbusters. Harry once again stares down danger but survives with the help of his two close friends. This time trouble presents itself in the form of escaped convict Sirius Black. Harry must turn to sympathetic professor Lupin for help.

Third Floor Quote:

It is suspected that Serious Black is in Hogwarts. They do a lock down and they search the Castle to see if they can find him. The old castle keeper named Mr. Filtch tells the headmaster, "I've searched the astronomy Tower and (???) but there is nothing there." Some other guy in the room says, "Yes, the Third Floor's clear too Sir."

I have listened to this section of the movie and I cannot make out what is said and that is why I have the question marks there. I listened again and again but could not make out what was said.

All of you advanced Harry Potter experts feel free to laugh at me.

Movie Title: I Robot
Date Released: 7/15/2004
Date Viewed: ~12/1/2004

Major Stars:

Will Smith	Alan Tudyk (Sonny the Robot)
Bruce Greenwood	Bridget Moynahan
Chi Mc Bride	Adrian Ricard

Movie Story:

It is the year 2035 and robots are common. They abide by the three laws of robotics. One particular cop is a bit techno phobic but he is driven to investigate the apparent suicide of a dear friend. In spite of what everyone tells him he suspects that a robot may be guilty of the crime and that a corrupt corporation may be on the verge of changing the robot - human relationship forever.

Third Grade Quote:

Will Smith goes to visit his grandmother and his face is roughed up and his grandmother asks him if he was beaten up by a certain Frank Murphy.

Will Smith's character says the following line to his grandmother Gee Gee. "Gee Gee, I haven't seen Frank Murphy since the 3rd grade."

Even though the third grade is not exactly the Third Floor I kept this here because I noticed in a lot of other movies people were mentioning the third this or the third that so I decided to put this one in the book. I also wanted to point out that I was taken out of Catholic school in the third grade and placed into public school. My God was that a shock to the system. It was like going from the military into Romper room. In public school, I kid you not; they had frogs, tadpoles, a fish tank, hamsters, and guinea pigs. They had finger paints and different colored chalk and all kinds of crêpe paper, scissors, and glue. It was sensory overload. My teacher was Miss May and it was like I died and had gone to heaven. I did leave behind my totally cool teacher at St. John's whose name was Miss Pontonski. She was a really great teacher.

Yo, Miss Pontonski, check it out, I'm writing a book!

Whenever I hear the word "Robot" I immediately think of "I Robot" the song by Alan Parsons Project. For all of you young people out there who have never heard of this song I recommend you find this song and download it to your iPad, or EG-7 matrix, or your K7-L-mE-PaD, or whatever technology is currently being used. It is a fantastic song.

Movie Title: Saint Ralph
Date Released: 9/11/2004
Date Viewed: ~2/11/2005

Major Stars:
Adam Butcher
Campbell Scott

Movie Story:
Ralph is your average teenager but he thinks in atypical ways. The biggest question he has is why has his mother fallen into a coma. The 14-year-old has decided to make a deal with God. The deal is if he wins the 1954 Boston marathon then his mother gets well. One teacher at his school who was a former runner agrees to be his coach and wants to encourage his dream.

300 Series Number:
Our main character the runner Ralph is taking a small Christmas tree to his mother's hospital room at Christmas. She is in a coma.

A bitchy nurse says, "Visiting hours are over."

He says, "My mother's room is in 309. I know where it is."

The nurse replies, "As I've already said, visiting hours are over."

After Ralph comes in second at the marathon he goes to see his Mom in her hospital room. You can see the 309 on the door very clearly. On a side note this number 309 has great significance for me. Route 309 is a major artery as a roadway all the way from Philadelphia to places far north, such as Quakertown. My father drove on Route 309 in his later years every day back and forth from work. He drove all the way from Quakertown to Center City to teach air conditioning and refrigeration at a technical school there. He drove a beautiful red Buick Skylark. He said it purred like a kitten. I ended up driving on Route 309 each day back and forth from my job as well. I have spent a lot of my time driving on good old Route 309.

Movie Title: Million Dollar Baby
Date Released: 12/14/2004
Date Viewed: ~5/14/2005

Major Stars:
Hilary Swank
Clint Eastwood
Morgan Freeman
Jay Baruchel

Movie Story:
Boxer wanna-be Maggie Fitzgerald wanders into the gym of trainer Frankie Dunn. Maggie is one determined young woman but Frankie doesn't train women and he never will. Frankie wasn't a good father and is estranged from his daughter. Frankie's heavy emotions make him that much more determined to not get involved with Maggie. Frankie's second in command finally wears down the old grouch and gets him to help Maggie to fulfill her dream to one day be a boxer.

300 Series Number:
Hilary Swank's character is severely injured and she lies in a bed in a hospital, room <u>301.</u>

As everybody knows this is a heartbreaking movie.

Movie Title: What's New, Pussycat
Date Released: 1/1/1965
Date Viewed: ~4/15/2006

Major Stars:
Peter Sellers
Peter O'Toole
Ursula Andress

Movie Story:
Skirt chaser Peter O'Toole is having trouble giving up his hedonistic lifestyle. He needs to settle down and marry his one true love. He seeks help from a psychiatrist played by Peter Sellers. The problem with the doctor though is that he is demented and is troubled by his own romantic shortcomings. There is a great deal of mad-cap 1960s style hijinks in this fast paced movie.

Third Floor Quote:
Peter O'Toole's and Peter Seller's characters are drunk and it is nighttime. They are outside a building and they are trying to get the attention of a woman that Seller's character loves. He says to O'Toole's character to throw a rock to hit the only lighted window. He says in German the numbers only, "1,2,3, that's the one, the 3rd one up there, that one."

***Special note:** This movie is out of chronological order. This movie was made in 1965, which, is well before the Third Floor rock phenomenon occurred. It is also before the movie Barfly occurred. Therefore it does not apply to either of my theories. But wait you say, I don't have a Barfly theory, but soon I will tell you about it.

Movie Title: Penelope
Date Released: 1/1/2006^
Date Viewed: ~5/1/2006

Major Stars:
Christina Ricci
James McAvoy
Reese Witherspoon

Movie Story:
This is a modern day fairy tale where a young woman is cursed with the nose of a pig. She is forced from shame and embarrassment to live her entire life in seclusion. Until one day when a special young man stumbles onto the scene and is able to overcome his urge to run from her deformity. They slowly get to know each other and he manages to convince her to embrace her inner beauty.

300 Series Number:
The curse of the nose is broken on her wedding day but not because of what you think. Her and her friend, played by Reese Witherspoon, go to a Halloween party at the very end of the movie and the guy that Penelope likes lives there. They are going to his room to see him. Penelope says, "Okay room 357." Reese's character says, "There it is." They are talking about the room number that the guy lives in. The camera does a close-up of the number on the door. It is 357 in big brass numbers.

I just realized something. Somebody out there might actually know the answer to this Third Floor mystery. If you do know the answer I must beg of you Sir or Madam to not reveal the answer. The revealing of the answer would completely ruin the mystery. I can't allow this to happen. This has to remain a mystery so that people will be intrigued and so that they will buy my book. I beg of you Sir or Madam to keep the answer covered up for at least three years after the book has been published. I mean holy smokes; I can't allow you guys to blow my book sales in Europe.

Movie Title: The Departed
Date Released: 10/5/1006
Date Viewed: ~3/5/2007

Major Stars:
Jack Nichlson
Matt Damon
Mark Wahlberg
Leonardo DiCaprio
Martin Sheen

Movie Story:
In order to take down South Boston's Irish Mafia the police have to send in one of their men to infiltrate the underworld. However the police don't know that the Irish Mafia has done the same thing. Here we have a multiple Oscar-winning crime thriller from Martin Scorsese. The undercover cop becomes a close confidant to the mob kingpin while on the other hand the career criminal becomes a high-ranking police officer. Eventually both sides find out that there are moles amongst them.

300 Series Number:
Martin Sheen plays a high-ranking state trooper official. He goes to meet DiCaprio's character who is an undercover agent. The bad guys follow Martin Sheen's character and they find him in the building and they throw him down to his death on the ground below. The address of that building is 344. In a much later scene DiCaprio and Matt Damon's undercover character both meet at that same address on the roof. Yet another 300 series number in a movie.

One time a few years after the Legendary rock band Third Floor had broken up and my friendship with Phil had healed he invited me to a party down at his and Blaine's place in Manayunk. He told me, "Hey you can come as Bukowski, or better yet you can leave as Bukowski." Very funny. He was making the point that it was obvious that if I came down to a party I would be leaving drunk. He was right.

What I should point out is that I went to a big Halloween party down there the fall after Bukowski died as Bukowski. I bought some old second hand clothes at a Thrift store. The clothes were old, from the 1970's era. I wore an old tie too. People kept asking me all night long, "Who are you supposed to be?" I had to tell them Bukowski but I did it in my best Mickey Rourke imitation voice. I was a hit that night and it was all done in Love to Charles somebody.

Movie Title: Oceans 13
Date Released: 6/7/2007
Date Viewed: ~11/7/2007

Major Stars:

George Clooney	Al Pacino	Matt Damon
Brad Pitt	Don Cheadle	Elliot Gould
Bernie Mac	Andy Garcia	

Movie Story:

Danny Ocean and his team of criminals are back and they are working up a plan more personal than ever. When the ruthless and treacherous casino owner Willy Bank doublecrossed Reuben Tishkoff causing Reuben to have a heart attack, Danny Ocean vows that his resourceful and creative team will do anything to bring down Mr. Bank. They even go so far as to seek help from one of their own enemies, Terry Benedict.

Third Floor Quote:

Matt Damon's character has to explain to Miss Sponder who is Al Pacino's second in command, who his client is and how he got all his money. His name is Mr. Weng and he made his fortune by purchasing air rights. Matt Damon's character explains it in this way to Miss Sponder. "Put it this way, try to build something larger than <u>three stories</u> in the Tiangjin Province, see if his name comes up in your database then."

Movie Title: Live Free or Die Hard
Date Released: 6/21/2007
Date Viewed: ~11/21/2007

Major Stars:
Bruce Willis
Mary Elizabeth Winstead
Timothy Olyphant
Justin Long

Movie Story:
John McClane is back and is as bad as ever. This time he is working for Homeland Security. He seeks out the services of a young brilliant hacker in order to go up against elements he is unfamiliar with. McLean has to take on a ring of Internet terrorist hell-bent on taking control of America's computer infrastructure.

Third Floor Quote:
They have said fourth floor twice already. I'm beginning to think I've got the wrong movie but then our scene comes around. McLean and the computer kid (Justin Long) are in the Woodlawn facility. McLean has kicked a guy down a metal stairwell. The bad guy is in bad shape. McLean leans over him and picks up his walkie-talkie and says to the bad guy lying there, "Where's my daughter?"

Timothy Olyphant's character is the mastermind bad guy. He says into his walkie-talkie, "Russo check in."

McLean says into the walkie-talkie, "Yeah, I think a Russo's on his way to meet your girlfriend dick head. Hold on a minute looks like he's coming around." The bad guy lying there on the floor bleeding tries to yell into the walkie-talkie,

"It's McLean, he's on the Third Floor, and the kid is...BANG!!!"

McLean shoots the bad guy before he can say anymore. McLean says into his walkie-talkie, "Get all that, that's right, I'm on the <u>Third Floor</u> but I'm coming to get cha."

(In a brief minute we find out that McLean didn't actually shoot the bad guy he just shot the gun near his head.)

I absolutely love Bruce Willis. I think he is an excellent actor with a wide range and few people can touch him when it comes to action movies. I was so glad that this movie had a Third Floor line in it. It was so cool to hear Bruce Willis say Third Floor with such conviction.

Guess what? I just remembered something. Way back in 1988 I went to visit my mom in California and I had a Third Floor cassette with me that was recorded at one of our parties, up the stairs, on the Third Floor. My mom lived in Studio City near Proost Avenue. I was a young, active; pot smoking hippie and I loved to play hackey sack. I told my Mom I was going out for walk around the neighborhood and I had my boom box with me and I was listening to the band. I came upon some California hippie dudes who were younger than me and they were playing hackey sack in a parking lot of a karate place on a bright sunny day.

I went over to those guys and asked if I could join in with their session of hackey sack. They were somewhat reluctant because I was six or seven years older than those guys and they probably thought that I might suck. Well they let me join in and were soon pleased to see that I was an excellent hackey sack player.

They asked me who I was and I told them I was visiting from the East Coast and I told them that I was an incredible drummer in a really hot band back East. I figured I wasn't doing anybody any harm by exaggerating how popular we were but I didn't go totally overboard. I did tell them, because I truly believed it to be true, that we were heading for a record deal. So I hung out with those guys and they decided I was cool enough to hang with them. I turned up my boombox so they could hear Third Floor more clearly. I was really happy when they said it was pretty good. It was a very satisfying feeling to feel that these young hipsters thought I was cool enough to hang with them. The one thing people from the East coast notice about California, is that the Sun is so bright. Everything thing seemed so much brighter. I was super happy when they fired up some doob-age.

I realized about a day later that I could make a tape or two for those guys and they could have some Third Floor out in California. My boombox had dual heads so I could make copies of tapes. So I bought some cassettes, which I did constantly in those days and made two copies of the Third Floor gig, which we called, "Live Concert" because we had all our songs down pat and could really blast through them. We played to a bunch of people in our bitchin flat. It was another one of our parties.

Keep in mind this is a lighthearted book. No one should get worked up over this book.

As silly as it seems I suspect those two cassettes that I gave to those young karate kids turned into an underground swell that led to thousands of people knowing about Third Floor the powerful East Coast conglomerate and as a result of our runaway popularity we influenced writers and directors of modern cinema to include the phrase Third Floor on a regular basis. You think I'm kidding right? You think I've gone crazy right? No, no my friend, I am dead serious.

OK, well crap! Do you have any better ideas?

Movie Title: I'm Not There
Date Released: 8/31/2007
Date Viewed: ~1/31/2008

Major Stars:
Cate Blanchett
Heath Ledger
Julianne Moore
Ben Whishhaw
Christian Bale

Movie Story:
Bob Dylan's life and work are taken on by six different characters that embody a different aspect of his life.

300 Series Number:
A little black kid is a key figure in the early part of the movie. I found this movie to be very strange and confusing. Is that little black kid supposed to be portraying the young Bob Dylan? If he is, doesn't anybody find that to be incredibly confusing? Well anyway there is a scene where the little black kid walks into a hospital and a nurse walks towards him and says, "May I help you?"

He responds by saying, "Flowers for Mr. Guthrie."

The nurse says, "<u>Room 300</u>, just set'em inside."

I hated this movie. I thought it was horrible. I love Cate and Christian. Don't get me wrong but jiminy crickets what a bad movie.

Daniel McTeigue

Movie Title: Camille   (60)
Date Released: 9/27/2008
Date Viewed: ~5/1/2008

Major Stars:
Sienna Miller
James Franco
David Carradine
Scott Glen

Movie Story:
Silas has had troubles with the law. Camille loves Silas no matter what. Camille's uncle is the local sheriff and he is forcing Silas to marry Camille. They decide a trip to Niagara Falls for the honeymoon is the right thing to do. Silas goes along with the plan even though he plans on escaping to Canada. There is one big problem though and that is that Camille dies in an accident but is still alive. Even though she is slowly decomposing she is having trouble coming to grips with her death.

Third Floor Quote:
At one point the police corner Silas and Camille in a hotel room. Camille plays dead because she already is dead. They wheel her out of the hotel room on the gurney. Silas is escaping by jumping down balcony layers. They run into each other in the hallway when the elevator door pops open. They flee down the hallway into a cement stairwell. Scott Glenn plays the role of Camille's uncle. He hears gunshots and runs up the cement stairwell while the police officer is running down the cement stairwell. They both run into each other and the door behind them says "3FL" Unbelievable!

How much do you want to bet that I'm **THE ONLY** guy on the whole planet who knows about this Third Floor movie mystery!

Movie Title: Tin Man
Date Released: 12/2/2007
Date Viewed: ~5/2/2008

Major Stars:
Zooey Deschanel
Alan Cummings
Richard Dreyfuss
Neal McDonough

Movie Story:
Set in the spirit of L. Frank Baum's classic, "The Wizard of Oz" this tale of Dorothy takes its own path down the yellow brick road. DG as Dorothy is a waitress and part-time student. She is caught up in the stories of other characters as they travel through the O.Z. (Outer Zone). This movie is a SyFy adaptation of the original tale as DG battles the sorceress Azkadellia with the help of her three friends, Glitch, Raw, and Wyatt Cain.

Third Floor Quote:
One of the main characters has had his brain removed. The evil witch removed his brain. It turns out his brain is being used to run a powerful device. The guy who is the Sheriff asks the main bad guy and the bad guy tells them where Glitch's brain can be located.

Glitch (Scare Crow): My marbles are in the tower?

Sheriff: "Where are they?

Bad guy: "Brain room, sub <u>level 3</u>."

Movie Title: Watchmen
Date Released: 7/1/2008
Date Viewed: ~12/01/2008

Major Stars:
Tom Stechschulte
Malin Akerman
Carla Gugino
Billy Crudup
Jeffrey Dean Morgan

Movie Story:
Back in the good old days comic book superheroes battled for what was viewed as right. These powerful figures shaped history even though they sometimes crossed the line of decency. But now their influence has faded while one of the now outlawed superheros investigates a possible conspiracy against his old friends. The actions of one godlike individual has a final plan that is truly cataclysmic.

300 Series Number:
In one of the very first scenes one of the premier characters called the comedian whose real name in the story is Edward Blake has the crap beaten out of him in a very violent and brutal fashion. He is thrown through a window of a high-rise building to his death. Right before the attacker enters his apartment he can see the shadows of the attackers feet under his door. In a flash the door flies open and the brutal attacker appears. There is no way to see that the number on the door is <u>300</u>! The only way that I saw it was by super slow scan method. They the creators of the "Third Floor Movie Mystery," tried to slip one past me. They almost got away with it. When the comedian was young he was one of the "Watchmen."

"I'm Not There" just had a 300 Room number. What the What?

Movie Title: Choke
Date Released: 9/26/2008
Date Viewed: ~2/26/2009

Major Stars:
Anjelica Huston
Sam Rockwell
Clark Gress
Kelly Mac Donald

Movie Story:
Imagine a man who risks choking to death just to earn a couple of sympathy related dollars. That is what Victor does. He is a sex addicted con-man who manages to pay for his mother's hospital bills by milking money out of those people who had saved him from choking to death. This guy needs some serious help.

Third Floor Quote:
Sam Rockwell's character Victor visits his mother who is in a nuthouse. She is played by Angelica Houston. She has dementia and doesn't know what's going on or whom he is. He shows up to try to feed her food.

Victor: "Hey where's Constance?"

Mother: "Upstairs, they took her this morning."

Victor: "Oh, well, she'll be back."

Mother: "Oh no she won't Fred. They take you up to the second floor you don't come back. If they take you up to the <u>Third Floor</u> you just better hope your plots paid up."

Movie Title: Alice
Date Released: 2009
Date Viewed: ~5/1/2009

Major Stars:
Caterina Scorsone
Kathy Bates
Harry Dean Stanton

Movie Story:
This is a re-imagining of Lewis Carroll's novel "Alice in Wonderland." Alice, as a young woman, descends into the underworld of Wonderland after her boyfriend is captured by the Queen of Hearts. The Hatter tries to maintain control in the realm as he battles a society called the White Rabbit.

Third Floor Quote:
Queen: You've had Jack for 3 days now and you got nothing from him.
Duchess: I just need a little more time, un-interrupted time.

White Knight: "I shall reach into the mist to lift the heavy veil that shrouds the Oracle. aaaahhhhhh oohoooh. Galadoom. baaauusheee. Down here take the second left at the stairs that lead up to the Third Floor then after the double doors take the walkway, third on the right over the fitted set to reception B and ask SHEEELAAA!!! maybe it's Shakeena. Come on. (Spoken very quickly)

This is the actor who did those crazy Coke-a-Cola commercials back in the 1980's.

This little scene spoken by the White Knight was very funny. I laughed my ass off.

The TF lines just keep coming and coming. It's incredible.

Movie Title: Che (Disk 2)
Date Released: 10/7/2008
Date Viewed: ~5/7/2009

Major Stars:

Benniceo Del Toro

Demian Bichir

Santiago Cabrera

Rodrigo Santoro

Catalina Sandino Moreno

Kahlil Mendez

Lou Diamond Philips

Movie Story:
Che, portrayed by Benniceo Del Toro, joins up with a band of Cuban exiles led by Fidel Castro. They travel to Cuba from Mexico in 1956. Within two years they generated popular support for their cause and a trained guerrilla army and toppled the US friendly regime of dictator Batista.

Third Floor Quote:
Che, played by Benniceo Del Toro, disguised as his father enters into Bolivia without any problems. He gets to his hotel the Copacabana. He gets in the elevator and goes up to the <u>Third Floor</u>. In the next instant there is a very tight close-up of a hotel door and the room number is <u>304</u>!

The other idea that I have as to why so many movies have the phrase Third Floor in them is that it may be a tribute to the legendary American poet / writer Charles Bukowski. I really think that this might be why this Third Floor scenario is occurring in so many movies. You have to go back to the movie the Barfly and that scene where Hank and Wanda are walking along the sidewalk at night and Wanda says, "My place is next. I'm up on the Third Floor."

It's not that one line of dialogue would set forth a commitment of so many writers to keep the phrase Third Floor alive and well in movies but it is the overall life achievements and tremendous influence that Bukowski had in literature and his huge personality in the LA area. For those of you who don't know who Charles Bukowski is I suggest you go to Amazon or your local bookstore and start buying and reading his books. You have over 40 books to choose from.

Bukowski was a legendary drinker and smoker. People in the LA area would go knock on his door at De Longpre Avenue and try to invite themselves in. Bukowski allowed for hundreds of such visits and the rule was you had to show up with a six pack of beer. Buk even had housewives from different states in the US fly out to meet him. He wasn't well known throughout the United States really until after the movie Barfly appeared. He was more popular in Germany then he was in the United States. There is no doubt in my mind that many young people who dreamed of becoming writers went and visited with Bukowski. He has had a huge impact on all poetry during his life and after his life.

I have several quotes of his from his letters and from his books where he mentions the Third Floor or 300 series apartments. I have these quotes scattered throughout the rest of the book. I have just one full poem to share. I am grateful that I have this full poem to share with you.

Book title: "The Pleasures of the Damned. Page 411
Charles Bukowski

"Goldfish"

my goldfish stares with watery eyes
into the hemisphere of my sorrow;
upon the thinnest of threads
we hang together,
hang hang hang
in the hangman's noose;
I stare into his place and
he into mine...
he must have thoughts,
can you deny this?
he has eyes and hunger
and his love too
died in January; but he is
gold, really gold, and I am gray
and it is indecent to search him out,
indecent like the burning of peaches
or the rape of children,
and I turn and look elsewhere,
but I know that he is there behind me,
one gold goblet of blood,
one thing alone
hung between the reddest cloud
of purgatory
and apt. no. 303.

god, can it be
that we are the same?

(1*)

Movie Title: Inkheart
Date Released: 12/17/2008
Date Viewed: ~5/17/2008

Major Stars:
Brendan Fraser
Andy Serkis
Sienna Guillory
Elizabeth Hope Bennett

Movie Story:
In this story certain very special people have the ability to bring words in books to life. A man loses his wife one night when thugs burst into their home. Now the husband and his daughter go searching for a precious book that may bring her back. There are forces on the dark side who want to control reality to their own ends. A secret is discovered that will aid the forces of light.

Third Door Quote:
When the travel party returns to the castle the flame guy, 'Dust Fingers' says to the lead male character played by Brendan Fraser, "When we get to the maids' quarters, Rees's room is the <u>third door</u> on the right when we go in the back."

Here is an example from one of his books whereby people are stopping over to visit him, Bukowski that is. This is from the book "Portions from a Wine Stained Notebook." Page102. Charles Bukowski.

"People keep coming through my door, talking to me; uninvited, they come and I listen, give them what I have to drink, and they leave. But those hours are not wasted -- man learns from man….." (2*)

Movie Title: Quantum of Solace
Date Released: 10/31/2008
Date Viewed: ~5/31/2009

Major Stars:
Daniel Craig
Judi Dench
Olga Kurylenko
Mathieu Amalric

Movie Story:
Quantum of Solace is a continuation of the adventures of James Bond after Casino Royale. Having been betrayed by Vesper, the woman he loved, 007 fights the urge to make his current mission personal. Bond is determined to uncover the truth. While Bond and M interrogate Mr. White he laughs at their naïveté as to how deep and dangerous the organization he works for really is.

300 Series Number:
Early in the movie MI6 analyzes the money in the wallet of the man 007 killed after the roof top foot chase. Money with similar serial numbers were deposited in a bank in Haiti. The bad guy's name is Mr. Slate. Bond travels to go see him. Mr. Slate is staying in the hotel Des Salines and he is staying in <u>Room 325</u>. We can see the numbers in black on the wall to the left of the door before 007 enters.

Book Title: Screams from the Balcony. Selected Letters. Page 31
Charles Bukowski
This is in a letter to Ann Bauman dated May 10, 1962

"Am sitting here having a beer and staring out the same window, three floors up, miles out into the nowhere of Hollywood."(3*)

Movie Title: Confessions of a Shopaholic
Date Released: 2/5/2009
Date Viewed: ~7/5/2009

Major Stars:
Isla Fisher
Joan Cusack
Hugh Dancy

Movie Story:
Rebecca Bloomwood is an energetic young woman who is really good at shopping. She lives in New York City and sees all with a glamorous eye. Her dream is to work for a fashion magazine but she can't get her foot in the door. Someone gives her the idea of taking a job as an advice columnist for a financial magazine published by the same company. The logic is, she is one step closer to her dream job. Unfortunately she can't seem to shake an annoying gentleman from the collection agency. You see her credit cards are a little bit maxed out.

Third Floor Quote:
Our main character, Becks, played by Isla Fisher, is riding up an escalator in her office building and she hears the voice of the collection agency guy who has been tormenting her. She goes running to an elevator. On the entrance of the elevator wall is the label <u>B*3</u>. Mr. Smeath, the collection agency guy gets in the elevator right after Becks does. The elevator stops on the <u>Third</u> <u>Floor</u> and random people get on and off.

Movie Title: Duplicity
Date Released: 3/19/2009
Date Viewed: ~8/18/2009

Major Stars:
Julia Roberts
Clive Owen
Paul Giamatti
Tom Wilkinson

Movie Story:
Two corporate spies who are romantically involved realize that they could team up together and deceive their respective employers and end up with boatloads of cash to retire on. But what they don't know is that their employers have a trick up their respective sleeves.

Third Floor Quote:
An employee is caught at night by two security guards with a document, which contains top-secret information. Julia Roberts and a coworker are called in by the night watch security guards. They want to re-secure the violated floors.

Julia Roberts: Is the area upstairs secure now?

The boss: Yeah, yeah are you sure there's nobody upstairs now?

Black haired guard: It's got to be cleared out before it's re-armed.

Julia Roberts: How long does that take?

Blonde haired guard: All <u>Three floors</u>, 20 minutes.

Here is another Bukowski Quote.
Book Title: Screams from the Balcony. Selected letters. pg 102
Charles Bukowski

This is a note written to a neighbor in the apartment building that he lives in.
Dated January 28, 1964

You knock on my floor when I type within hours. Why in the hell don't you keep your stupid t.v. set down at 10:30 tonight? I don't complain to managers, but it seems to me that your outlook is very one sided.

H. Bukowski
Apt. #303

Do you see how Bukowski lived in a 300 series apartment number? (4*)

Movie Title: The Front Page (70)
Date Released: 12/1/1974
Date Viewed: ~8/24/2009

Major Stars:

Jack Lemmon	Vincent Gardenia	Harold Gould
Charles Durning	Walter Matthau	David Wayne
Carol Burnett	Herb Edelman	Susan Sarandon
Allen Garfield	Austin Pendleton	Dick O' Neill
John Korkes	Martin Gabel	

Movie Story:

The Front Page is a comedy classic from director Billy Wilder made in 1974. Jack Lemmon plays journalist Johnson who is suffering from burnout and wants to finally quit his stressful job. On the other hand his boss played by Walter Matthau doesn't want him to quit no way, no how. The movie features a true All-Star cast. The two men battle it out.

Third Floor Quote:

Susan Sarandon's character is riding in a Cab and she is stopping off to pick up her fiancé played by Jack Lemmon. He is supposed to be waiting outside.

Susan Sarandon says to the taxicab driver, "He said he'd be waiting."

The cabbie says, "You want me to go get him?"

Ms. Sarandon says, "Would you please. Third Floor press room."

***Special Note: This movie was released in 1974 so it obviously was not influenced by the underground Third Floor rocks legends theory and it is also not influenced by the Charles Bukowski theory.

Movie Title: An American in Paris
Date Released: 10/4/1951
Date Viewed: ~8/28/2009

Major Stars:

Gene Kelley   Oscar Levant

Leslie Caron   Georges Guetary

Movie Story:

Gene Kelly plays the role of Jerry Mulligan an energetic American expatriate living in Paris while trying to make it as a painter. His friend Adam (Oscar Levant) is a concert pianist who happens to be a friend of the famous French singer Henri Baurel (Georges Guétary). A wealthy woman portrayed by Nina Foch appreciates Jerry's art and takes an interest in helping to support him.

Third Floor Quote and 300 Series Number:

In the very first scene there is a camera showing the outside of a building. They show the activity going on in the second-floor apartment and then the camera scans up to where Gene Kelly is living which is clearly the <u>Third Floor</u> but, they don't say it.

Gene Kelly's character goes to the rich woman's apartment. She opens the door in her hotel room. It is apartment <u>311</u>. You can see it clearly on the door when Gene Kelly walks in.

***Special Note: This movie was released in 1951 so it obviously was not influenced by the underground Third Floor rocks legends theory and it is also not influenced by the Charles Bukowski theory. I want to include these movies anyway just because it adds to the fun. It adds to the number of movies in the whole charade.

Movie Title: State of Play
Date Released: 4/17/2009
Date Viewed: ~9/17/2009

Major Stars:
Russell Crowe
Ben Affleck
Rachael McAdams
Helen Mirren

Movie Story:
U. S. Congressman Stephen Collins is highly skilled and is the future of his political party. He serves as the chairman overseeing a committee on defense spending. Many in his party see him as a contender for the presidential race. All is fine until his research assistant / mistress is murdered and hidden secrets are revealed.

Third Floor Quote:
Russell Crowe's character says to Rachel Mc Adams's character as they are walking out of their newspaper office at night, "You ever been to DC hospital? Well don't worry it's easy. All right, there's a uniformed officer on the <u>Third Floor</u>, ICU. Write it down, you have a pen. OK, uniformed officer's name is Brown, OK, <u>Third Floor</u> ICU."

Book title: Screams from the Balcony. Selected letters. pg 138
Charles Bukowski

This is from a letter from early April 1965 to Douglas Blazek.

"I was staring pretty much at pretty knife blades way up high in a 3rd. floor place…" (5*)

Movie Title: Spring Breakdown
Date Released: 6/2/2009
Date Viewed: ~11/2/2009

Major Stars:
Amy Poehler
Rachel Dratch
Parker Posey
Amber Tamblyn

Movie Story:
Three women in their 30s who never got to sow their wild oats at spring break when they were young head to a popular spring break location and try to get wild and crazy. You're never too old to party.

Third Floor Quote:
All three main characters Amy Poehler, Parker Posey, and Rachel Dratch are about to check into a hotel down at spring break in San Padre and the hotel is a Four Seasons. It turns out the Hotel is called the Four Seasone's. It is a total dive. The check in clerk is a big-breasted blonde who is on her 18th spring break. One of our main characters says, "OK checking in, Becky Saint Jermaine." The hotel clerk says, "That's right, got cha'll in a suite on the <u>Third Floor</u>."

Why? Why? Why did this happen? Why were they checked into the Third Floor Suite? How come they were not checked into the 5th floor suite? I'll tell you why because everybody knows that if you're at a place and you plan or doing some serious partying you stay on the Third Floor. And that's what's up!

This is a horrible movie by the way. You should not watch this movie. Although, it was great to hear the big blonde say Third Floor with such gusto.

Here is another example of the average Joe or Jane stopping over to visit Buk unannounced. Charles Bukowski: "Portions from a Wine Stained Notebook" page 120

"There are others. They keep coming. All with their special brand of talk or living. I've drawn some good ones, these Los Angeles characters, and I suppose they'll keep coming. I don't know why people bring me themselves. I never go anywhere." (6*)

My belief is that some of these random people are writers themselves who have gone on to write for TV shows and major movie studios. They were there in the presence of Bukowski back in the day and they are keeping his memory alive with this super top-secret "Third Floor Movie Mystery." But, only the writers know about it.

Movie Title: Away we Go
Date Released: 6/5/2009
Date Viewed: ~11/5/2009

Major Stars:

Maya Rudolph
John Krasinski
Catherin O'Hara
Josh Hamilton

Carmen Ejogo
Maggie Gyllenhaal
Jeff Daniels

Movie Story:
Verona and Burt moved to Colorado to be close to Burt's parents since Verona was pregnant. They are both stunned to find out Burt's aloof parents plan on moving to Belgium. Neither Verona or Burt want to stay in Colorado now that their support structure is gone. They proceed to set out on a journey to find a new place to live where they have friends or relatives. On their journey of discovery they realize it's more about finding out what type of parents they are going to be rather than where they are going to make their home.

300 Series Number:
John Krainski's character says to a woman as they are walking on a college campus, "Excuse me, do you know where Ellen Fisher Herinn's office is?" The woman who is a stranger to them says, "Ellen Fisher Herrin, yes I do know as a matter of fact, she's in William Stone Hall, room 340, about half way down."

So once again folks we have another 300 series room number in a movie, dum-dum-dum!

I have found another passage, which adds credence that Buk was visited by an endless array of people, characters from around L.A.

This is from "Portions from a Wine Stained Notebook." This is from the story "The L.A. Scene," page 112. Charles Bukowski.

"In Los Angeles it is possible to live in total isolation until they find you, and they will find you. And drink with you for days and nights, and talk for days and nights. And when they are gone, others will come along. One doesn't mind the women, of course, but the others are definitely consumers of the soul." (7*)

Movie Title: The Invention of Lying
Date Released: 9/14/2009
Date Viewed: ~2/14/2010

Major Stars:
Ricky Gervais
Jennifer Garner
Louis C.K.
Philip Seymour-Hoffman

Movie Story:
This story takes place in a world where the idea of lying doesn't exist. An unhappy man changes the course of his life significantly when he invents lying to get ahead.

300 Series Number:
Early in the movie we find out that Ricky Gervais's character Mark Bellisen is being evicted from his apartment. We can see the door to apartment 328 over the apartment manager's shoulder. Later in the movie when Anna is at Mark's apartment Louis C.K. comes over with pizza and when he comes we can see that Mark lives in apartment 329!

Movie Title: It's Complicated
Date Released: 12/25/2009
Date Viewed: ~5/25/2010

Major Stars:
Meryl Streep
Alec Baldwin
Steve Martin
Lake Bell

Movie Story:
Jane and Jake Adler have been divorced for 10 years. They see each other at their son's college graduation and unexpectedly end up sleeping together. The problem is Jake is married and Jane has just met her architect Adam and there seems to be sparks there. Now Jane's life is complicated and she has to figure out what she wants to do.

Third Floor Quote:
When the family is in the New York City hotel they all meet at the elevator, which is on the <u>Third Floor</u>. Jack Kevorkian, of all people, gets off the elevator in front of them.

Book Title: Living on Luck. Selected letters. Pg. 15
Charles Bukowsk

This is in a letter to John William Corrington dated February 23, 1961

"What his name is doesn't matter and you can multiply him by the hairs of grass that look so sickly up at me from my third floor rented window." (8*)

Do you see what I'm saying? Do you see how many references he makes to his third floor living space. Think of all of the writers that have held Bukowski in tremendous high esteem. Imagine all of the writers that have either visited him, or met him in bars, or out at the horse track, or have been inspired by his writing from far distances away.

Whenever I hear the phrase: from a distance away I always think of "The Larch." If you don't know what this means, look to 1970's English humor.

Movie Title: Fame
Date Released: 1/1/2009
Date Viewed: ~6/1/2009

Major Stars:

Megan Mullally   Kherington Payne
Kay Panabaker   Walter Perez
Nuturi Naughton   Asher Book

Movie Story:
An updated version of the 1980 musical, which centered on the students of the New York Academy of Performing Arts

300 Series Number:
A petite white girl who is incredibly cute is obviously intimidated by the big New York City. She gets to school late.

She asks a guy, "Do you know where room <u>310</u> is."
The guy kind of ignores her.

Another guy says, "Are you lost?"

She says, "Uhh, Uhh a yeah actually I'm looking for room <u>310</u>, Mr. Dodds class, acting."

He says, "Yeah, actually I think I think they're that way."

Movie Title: Leap Year
Date Released: 1/8/2010
Date Viewed: ~6/8/2010

Major Stars:
Amy Adams
Matthew Goode
John Lithgow
Adam Scott

Movie Story:
An American woman has a plan to propose to her reluctant boyfriend on Leap Day in Ireland. She follows him over there when he goes on a business trip. Her plan faces some major hurdles when bad weather and other problems arise. She has to be in Dublin on February 29 for the whole scheme to work out. She travels through the Irish countryside with the help of an innkeeper who slowly wears down her snobbish veneer.

A Number 3 Scenario:
The first line spoken in the movie is some real estate guy saying to Amy Adams character, "So happy you're here, this is the 3rd open house and not one bite." Amy's character Anna travels to Ireland and when she's there she stays in a little bar / hotel and her room number is 3! She stays in Room 3.

Oh my God. Why does this keep happening? It's really unbelievable. It's been fun for me though as the totally crazy Third Floor drummer guy.

Amy Adams is such a cutie pie but so many Hollywood actresses are. I love so many of them that it would be too long of a list to write.

Movie Title: The Repo Men
Date Released: 3/19/2010
Date Viewed: ~8/19/2010

Major Stars:
Jude Law
Forest Whitaker
Alice Braga
Live Schreiber

Movie Story:
In the not too distant future artificial human organs can be bought but if you can't afford the high price you can buy on credit. However if you can't make the payments Repo men may come by and re-claim the organ. What happens when a Repo man needs an artificial organ?

Third Floor Quote:
Jude Law's character gets out of an elevator and you have to look really fast to the right to see a #3 on the elevator door. Not on the front of the door but on the part that touches the other door when they close. You will have to do a 'pause scan' to see it.

When he walks out of the elevator you have to look to the left very quickly to see a large #3 in white. He is walking out of an elevator that is on the Third Floor!

You go Up the Stairs
    Up the Stairs
    To the Third Floor
    To the Third Floor

Movie Title: Killers   (80)
Date Released: 4/4/2010
Date Viewed: ~09/4/2010

Major Stars:
Katherine Heigl
Tom Selleck
Ashton Kutcher
Alex Borstein

Movie Story:
An elite assassin decides he has had enough of his stressful career. He meets a beautiful woman and decides he will settle down with her. The problem is some of his enemies don't like the idea of him riding off into the sunset. They like the idea of cutting his life short.

Third Floor Quote:
Tom Selleck's character is talking to a hotel clerk at the counter. "You have my wife and I on the second floor and my daughter on the third when I specifically booked adjacent rooms."

Tom's character, the father, says to the clerk, "Third Floor, we'd like an ocean view."

In a later scene Spencer's spy boss says to him, "Meet me in the room. I'm in room 114." This is just a little side note but our old Third Floor Studea's address was 141. This is something only I would notice.

Movie Title: Karate Kid
Date Released: 6/10/2010
Date Viewed: ~11/10/2010

Major Stars:

Jaden Smith   Yu Rong-Guang
Jackie Chan   Xu Ming
Taraji P. Henson

Movie Story:

Dre Parker was a happy 12 year old kid living in Detroit with his mom. Unfortunately his mother's company has decided to transfer her to China. Dre meets a pretty girl there named Mei Ying but the boys in the neighborhood don't like the idea of their friendship at all. Dre is harassed by the class bully, Cheng. Dre is down on his luck but makes friends with the maintenance man Mr. Han who happens to be a kung fu master. Mr. Hahn trains Dre and he puts the emphasis on maturity and inner calm. Dre develops the confidence needed to survive in his neighborhood and wins the respect Mei Ying.

300 Series Number:

The first scene of the karate kid our main character, played by Jaden Smith, and his mom are leaving their home and moving to China. They leave their apartment building and the address, which you can see behind them is a big number <u>368</u>. That's a 300 series number.

They arrive in China at their new apartment building and they're out in front and a blonde haired kid walks up to "Dre" and says, "Oh yeah, you you must be the new dude in <u>305</u>. I'm Harry." Dre answers back, "Hey, what's up I'm Dre."

Dre has to find Mr. Hahn who is played by Jackie Chan. Mr. Hahn is the maintenance man and Dre has to find him because his mom is trying to take a shower but the water is not hot. Dre has to search around and he says apartment <u>305</u> to several people.

Dre gets into a fight his first day on the local playground. He returns home to his new apartment and there is an extreme close-up of the number <u>305</u> on the door.

Why does the director take the time to do a close up of the <u>number 305</u>?

Movie Title: Takers
Date Released: 8/26/2010
Date Viewed: ~1/26/2011

Major Stars:
Chris Brown
Matt Dillon
Hayden Christensen
Michael Ealy

Movie Story:
A team of highly skilled bank robbers pull off another job and live the high life from their riches. As they are thinking about what their next job will be one of their former members nicknamed "Ghost" is released from prison and gets back with the crew. He tries to convince them that their next job should be a heist on an armored car carrying $20 million. What they don't know is that a dangerous police officer is tracking them closely.

A Number 3 Scenario:
Matt Dillon's characters name is Jack. The opening scene is two guys sitting in a car. The passenger takes a phone call on his cell. He answers, 'Yo D-Mac what's up?" The fact that he calls him D- Mac is funny to me because off and on throughout my life people would sometimes call me D-Mac or Danny Mac. Jack continues by saying, "Yeah I'm interested, What-a-ya-got for me? Hatians, Boyle Heights, yeah I know the place, 3B!" A few minutes later him and his partner kick in the door of apartment 3B.

Here is my big idea for the Bukowski conspiracy. This is it folks. This is what I have come up with after many years of thinking about this. Again people may say I'm crazy and that I have lost my mind and that I need to be placed into a nuthouse. But, that is okay with me. As long as they have high quality nutcrackers I wouldn't mind being sent to a nut house.

So my theory is this. Dinosaurs are skinny at one end, fat in the middle, and skinny at the other end. No wait, wait. That's not my theory. That is someone else's theory.

My big theory is that Charles Bukowski is a legend and he had a huge influence on up and coming writers in the LA area. For those of us who are huge Bukowski fans we know that he was a larger than life character. He wrote a script for one Hollywood movie and it is more of an independent movie than a big blockbuster movie but to fans of Bukowski it is priceless.

I believe that a portion of Hollywood script writers have said to each other, "Let's have our own secret code in movie scripts that pay homage to the legendary Buk." A certain group of writers agreed and they have maintained the introduction of the line Third Floor to their scripts or occasionally they'll use a 300 series number for an address or room number. The only people who know about this are the writers who took this secret pact to maintain their tribute to one of the greatest American writers of all time.

As a result of my intense level of drumming and as a result of the love I had for my band and the incredible music we made I had the phrase Third Floor on the brain and so I noticed this phrase being mentioned in movies whereas normal people would never have noticed.

I am currently hoping that I'm going to win some million-dollar prize pool as a result of being the person who figured out the conspiracy. God I hope there is a prize pool.

So I am either brilliant for figuring this out or it is all just a huge coincidence that all of these movies mention Third Floor or have a 300 series number in them.

I sure hope I'm right about the script writers' conspiracy.

Movie Title: Going the Distance
Date Released: 9/2/2010
Date Viewed: ~2/3/2011

Major Stars:
Drew Barrymore
Christina Applegate
Justin Long

Movie Story:
Erin's (Drew Barrymore) sharp wit and colorful personality charm the pants off newly single Garrett (Justin Long) over beer, bar trivia, and hanging out the next morning. The two are caught up in a rapid romance. Neither of them are super serious about the relationship because both of them know that Erin heads to San Francisco soon. As time passes the bond of the relationship grows and after six weeks neither of them is sure if they want the relationship to end. Two of Garrett's friends, both guys, tease him endlessly about his new girlfriend.

A Number 3 Scenario:
Apartment <u>3A</u> is in the opening scene.

Special note: the main character's name is Dan and there is also a Hugh character. My name is Dan and my middle name is Hugh. I also had a brother named Hugh and an uncle named Hugh.

Here is one more quote that proves many people randomly visited Charles Bukowski without announcing their arrival. In this quote he points out that he was visited by other writers.

This is also from "Portions from a Wine Stained Notebook. Page 122.

"Other writers begin to arrive, to knock on the door, bringing in their sixpacks. I never visited them but they did arrive. I drank with them and talked but they brought me very little and had a way of arriving at the wrong time. The ladies arrived to but they usually brought along something more useful than literary chit chat. Bad writers have a proclivity to talk about writing; good writers will talk about anything else but that. Very few good writers arrived." (9*)

Movie Title: Burlesque
Date Released: 11/23/2010
Date Viewed: ~4/23/2010

Major Stars:

Cher

Eric Dane

Christina Aguilera

Cam Gigandet

Stan Tucci

Julianne Hough

Kristen Bell

Movie Story:

The Burlesque Lounge has seen better days. Tess, a retired dancer who is now owner of the club, struggles to keep the venue financially stable. The lounge's performers are becoming increasingly stressed by their personal problems. There is also the problem of the wealthy businessman who was trying to buy the property from Tess. In walks Ali, a small town girl from Iowa who has a dream of one day being a singer. She is first hired as a waitress but soon gets her shot at being a performer. No one was prepared for the power of her talent.

300 Series Number:

Christina Aquilera's character is Ali. Her apartment gets robbed. So she goes to stay at one of her co-workers' apartment. The guy who lives there has the character name of Jack. He lives in apartment 316. So once again we have another 300 series room or door in the movie. In the morning when it is raining very hard Ali decides that she can't stay and that she has to leave. She runs out into the rain. Jack opens up the door behind her and yells out to her and you can see a close-up look at the number 316.

Movie Title: Little Fockers
Date Released: 12/21/2010
Date Viewed: ~5/21/2011

Major Stars:

Robert DeNiro	Barbara Streisand	Harvey Keitel
Owen Wilson	Teri Polo	
Ben Stiller	Blythe Danner	
Dustin Hoffman	Jessica Alba	

Movie Story:
Ten years have gone by and Greg and Pam have had two little Fockers and Greg has had to jump over countless hurdles but he has finally gotten the approval of his high strung father-in-law Jack. Greg and Pam have been having a little bit of money trouble so Greg takes a job moonlighting for a drug company. Father Jack gets suspicious when he thinks he sees Greg acting strangely. Greg grows increasingly annoyed with the constant pressure from Jack and the tension leads to a showdown.

300 Series Number:
The super hot pharmaceutical drug representative Andy, played by Jessica Alba, is hugging the dad / nurse character played by Ben Stiller and they are in a hospital. The wife Pam played by, Teri Polo, walks around the corner and is very surprised to see her husband being hugged by this super hot lady. Robert DeNiro shows up and he is the father of Pam. Then Owen Wilson's character, Kevin, shows up as well. There is a long scene played out and the whole time there is a room marker there and the number is 344. Once again here we have another 300 series room number prominently displayed during a movie scene.

There is something super spooky going on here or perhaps just a total coincidence but I just saw "The Departed" a few days ago, as I am re-watching many of these movies, and in that movie two very prominent scenes take place at the address of a building which is 344. If you recall Martin Sheen's character is killed at that address. What the Hell!

Movie Title: X-Men First Class
Date Released: 5/24/2011
Date Viewed: ~10/24/2011

Major Stars:

James McAvoy	Jennifer Lawrence	Zoe Kravitz
Michael Fassbender	Kevin Bacon	Alex Gonzalez
Ross Bryne	Oliver Platt	Jason Flemyng
January Jones	Nicholas Hoult	

Movie Story:

Charles Xavier and Erik Lensherr were once young men who were friends. They both explored together as they discovered their powers for the first time. Well before they became arch enemies they worked together with other mutants to stop the greatest threat the world has ever known.

Third Floor Quote:

Prof. Xavier as a young man talks to some members of the CIA. They throw him out of the room. The young female CIA spy, Lori, talks to him outside in the hallway. He is pretending to drink water from a water fountain but he is actually communicating to her via mental telepathy.

He says to her, "I'm as interested in this Sebastian Shaw as you are and if you still want my help, meet me on the <u>Third Floor</u> of the parking garage."

Movie Title: Kung Fu Panda
Date Released: 5/25/2011
Date Viewed: ~10/25/2011

Major Stars:

Jack Black	Dustin Hoffman	Michael Clarke Duncan
Angelina Jolie	Jackie Chan	Randall Duk Kim
Gary Oldman	Lucy Lui	James Hong
Seth Rogen	David Cross	Ian McShane
Dan Fogler		

Movie Story:

Po is now living his dream as The Dragon Warrior, protecting the Valley of Peace alongside his friends and fellow kung fu masters, The Furious Five. Little does Po know that there is a horrible villain who is poised to attack. Po's life of awesomeness will be threatened. This horrible villain has a secret weapon that is unstoppable and will enable him to conquer China and destroy kung fu. It is up to Po and the Furious Five to face this outlaw and destroy this horrible weapon. Po's traumatic childhood may hold some answers to help him defeat such a powerful foe.

Third Floor Quote:

"I threw up a little on the <u>Third Floor</u>. Someone might want to clean that up." So says Po, Jack Black's character.

This is an absolutely great quote considering how much beer and other drugs were consumed on the real THIRD FLOOR, by some people. I love this quote like crazy.

I would love to, in real life, share the sacred archives of Third Floor with Jack Black. He is one guy who is actively attuned to the GOD rays of Rock Knowledge.

Movie Title: Transformers: Dark of the Moon
Date Released: 6/28/2011
Date Viewed: ~11/28/2011

Major Stars

Shia LaBeouf	John Malkovich	Frances McDormand
Josh Duhamel	Tyrese Gibson	Hugo Weaving
Leonard Nimoy	Ken Jeong	Rosie Huntington-Whiteley

Movie Story:

Sam Witwicky is not a young teenager anymore. The march of time is moving him into adulthood. He continues to grapple with the idea that he is a human ally of Autobot-leader Optimus Prime. This story centers around an ongoing space race between the USSR and the USA. There is the potential that there was a crashed and hidden Transformer on the moon.

Third Floor Quote, a 300 Series Number and a Number 3 Scenario:

Throughout the movie there are multiple meetings between military people and the Autobots. They show repeatedly a big sign, which is painted on the wall and it says E North 317. Here is another example of a 300 series number prominently displayed in a movie. Why is this happening?

In one scene the Autobots are being placed on a space shuttle type transport. Shai LaBouf's character is saying goodbye to Optimus Prime and there is shown a cement pillar with a number 3 clearly painted on it. Shai's Autobot friend Bumblebee is standing next to the pillar. It is a clearly painted number 3 my friend.

Towards the end of the movie when the humans are getting closer to attacking the main building in the Chicago area, which they have to destroy, a few different US military groups run into each other on the street. The main commander yells out the command, "Yoh, you guys, follow that ground team, go and *secure* the Third Floor, we're going to 45."

Movie Title: Larry Crowne
Date Released: 6/30/2011
Date Viewed: ~11/30/2011

Major Stars:
Tom Hanks
Julia Roberts
Cedric the Entertainer

Movie Story:
Due to a stagnant economy and new rules imposed by a heartless corporation a middle-aged man loses his job. Forced into his dire predicament he signs up for some courses at the local college. As a result of interacting with the young students and his pretty teacher the man reinvents himself.

300 Series Number:
Tom Hanks's character, Larry Crowne, drops off Julia Robert's character Mrs. Tainot at her apartment one night. Mrs. Tainot lives in Apt. 325.

Yeah it's the same old story, another 300 series apartment number.

Here is some more Bukowski information to support my main theory that many Hollywood script-writers include the phrase Third Floor in their movies because they are all fans of Charles Bukowski and that they have a secret pact whereby they pay tribute to the man in this secretive way.

This quote is from the book from Neeli Cherkovski called Bukowski: A Life. This passage is from page 118.

"Gazing out onto Mariposa Street from his shabby front room, Hank wrote "The State of World Affairs From a Third Floor Window." His writing desk faced the window and as he stared outside long enough to gather an image, "… A girl dressed in a light green sweater, blue shorts, long black stocking…" Appeared." (10*)

So here is another example of a "Third Floor" phrase from a Bukowski passage. Imagine the number of young writers who got to visit the Legend in his Third Floor apartment.

Movie Title: The Hedgehog   (90)
Date Released: 8/9/2011
Date Viewed: ~1/9/2012

Major Stars:
Garance Le Guillermic
Josiane Balasko
Togo Igawa
Anne Brochet

Movie Story:
Paloma is a serious and very intelligent but troubled 11-year-old girl who has decided to kill herself on her 12th birthday. She is bored to tears by the interaction of her family members in their apartment. Even at a young age she is aware of the absurdity of the human condition. She has a movie camera and she documents many of her observations. One day Paloma has a close interaction with the buildings grumpy superintendent and she is intrigued by her. A new tenant moves in and he is Japanese and he is obviously a learned man. Both of these new companions give her life hope.

Third Floor Quote:
One of our main characters the superintendent, René, is going up the steps to visit Mr.Ozu when she passes an old woman who is sitting on a comfortable bench.

The old woman says, "Are those cakes?"

The superintendent responds, "Yes, a surprise delivery."

The old woman then shouts out with some disdain, "Why did you remove the flowers?"

René stops walking and turns to the old woman and says to her, "Mrs. deBroglie, this is the first floor. Your apartment is on the <u>Third Floor</u>."

When René is in Mr. Ozu's apartment he says to René, "It's the third door on the right." He is pointing out which room is the movie room. They are going to watch a movie together.

This is a very special movie. I don't think the title of the movie does the movie justice. The young girl who is a main character is a great artist. This movie has a very explosive ending, which is part of the reason that it is such a good movie. This is one of those movies that you find yourself thinking about weeks and months after seeing it. This is a 4 star movie.

Movie Title: Killer Elite
Date Released: 9/23/2011
Date Viewed: ~2/23/2012

Major Stars:
Jason Statham
Robert DeNiro
Clive Owen
Dominic Purcell

Movie Story:
Based on a shocking true story, Killer Elite pits two of the world's best operatives against a brilliant leader of a secret military society. Danny is an ex-special Ops agent and his long time mentor is Hunter. Hunter is captured and Danny reluctantly must go to free his old teacher. The Middle Eastern enemies are not going to make it so easy. This story takes place in Australia, Paris, London, and the Middle East.

A Number 3 Scenario:
Robert DeNiro's character, Hunter, is captured after accepting big money and trying to run with the money without doing the job. Jason Statham's character, Danny, is determined to get his old friend and mentor out of capture. Towards the end of the movie DeNiro is put in charge of keeping Danny's girlfriend safe. DeNiro has to shoot the big black guy who lines up their jobs. He wants a cut of the money, which he is due. DeNiro shoots this guy at a train station where Danny's girlfriend was. The big black dude was going to kidnap her for leverage. The guy is shot in the leg and struggles to a bench. As DeNiro approaches him and picks up the huge guy's gun which is lying on the ground there is a placard with a number 3 above them. When DeNiro's character walks away you can see the number 3 placard or sign again.

The director made sure that the sign was in plain view.

I wish I could share whole Bukowski poems with you the reader but it can get expensive to get permission to copy whole poems. The last line of this poem is hugely ironic because Charles Bukowski is one of the greatest writers of the last century and many of the things that he has written have turned to gold. The last line of the poem said that everything Bukowski touched turned to shit.

Here is another excerpt from a poem by Bukowski, which has him going to a 300 series room. This poem is from the book, "The Last Night of the Earth Poems." It is from page 111.

"Everything you touch"

"Or in Los Angeles, coming in from your shipping clerk job at an auto parts warehouse, taking the elevator up to 319 to find your woman sprawled out on the bed, drunk at 6 p.m." (11*)

Movie Title: The Ides of March
Date Released: 10/7/2011
Date Viewed: ~3/7/2012

Major Stars:

George Clooney	Evan Rachel Wood	Jeffrey Wright
Ryan Gosling	Paul Giamatti	
Marisa Tomei	Philip Seymour Hoffman	

Movie Story:
A young man with high ideals is on the staff of a presidential candidate. He is exposed to a lot of dirty underhanded tactics within the political dealings. A young woman is a casualty of the unpleasantness. The young man is drug down into the ugliness and has to become tough in order to survive

Third Floor Quote:
Ryan Gosling's character named Steven goes to the hotel where the young woman Molly is staying after he was not hired by the character played by Paul Giamatti. He walks into her room and you can see a female body lying on the ground. He walks slowly across the room with a look of dread on his face. There is a African American hotel worker on the phone sitting on the bed. The hotel worker says to Steven, "Do you know her? She's gone." The hotel employee then says to the people on the phone, "Um, um, I'm sorry what. Oh yes I can hear em now. We're on the Third Floor."

The number keeps growing and growing. This is not some sort of coincidence. There are just way too many movies.

Movie Title: Underworld: Awakening
Date Released: 1/20/2012
Date Viewed: ~6/20/2012

Major Stars:

Kate Beckinsale

Stephen Rea

Michael Ealy

Theo James

India Eisley

Charles Dance

Movie Story:

A vampire named Selene was held in a coma-like state for 15 years. When she escapes she eventually learns that she has a 14 year old vampire/Lycan daughter named Nissa. Selene is in a battle to stop BioCom from creating super Lycans that will kill them all.

A Number 3 and Level 3 Quote:

When Kate Beckinsale's character is planting the explosives along the elevator shaft, on all of the different floors in one brief moment we see a number 3 on the inside yellow lights of the elevator then we see a white number 3 painted on a steel girder. The top cop helps Kate Beckinsale's character because his wife had become a vampire. He watched her burned to death in the sunlight in their home. The top cop and Kate drive to the facility where her vampire daughter is being held. The cop says to Kate via walkie-talkie that, "I'm here, I got movement on a van on parking level 3, no sign of the girl."

Movie Title: One for the Money
Date Released: 1/27/2011
Date Viewed: ~6/27/2012

Major Stars:
Katherin Heigl
Debbie Reynolds
John Leguizamo
Sherri Shepard

Movie Story:
Stephanie Plum, an unemployed lingerie buyer is out of work and convinces her bail bondsman cousin, Vinny to give her a shot at being a bounty hunter. She gets her first assignment and she has to track down a former cop named Joe Morelli. He is on the run for murder and he happens to be the man who broke her heart years before. She gets help from her friends and is really lucky to get help from a top-notch bounty Hunter named Ranger. As time goes by her skills improve.

Third Floor Quote:
Morelli was "holded-up" on the <u>Third Floor</u> of the Gold Corp. factory.

(He was the main big bad guy)

Movie Title: Catch 44
Date Released: 12/9/2011
Date Viewed: ~5/9/2012

Major Stars:
Bruce Willis
Malin Akerman
Nikki Reed
Forest Whitaker
Deborah Ann Woll

Movie Story:
The lives of three female assassins take a horrible turn when their charming boss convinces them to take one last job. They all end up in a small diner when chaos erupts. Soon everyone has a gun pointed at them including a crazy hitman, a worn-out trucker, and a delusional short order cook.

Third Floor Quote:
A guy is trying to pick up one of the main female characters. It is the woman with the blond hair. He says, "Why don't we go back to my place at <u>Third Floor</u> and Fairfield."

Comment: this is kind of weird because it means the street name is Third-Floor. I listened to it several times and that is what it sounded like.

Movie Title: The 3 Stooges
Date Released: 4/13/2012
Date Viewed: ~9/13/2012

Major Stars:
Chris Diamantopoulous
Will Sasso   Sofia Vergara   Jennifer Hudson
Sean Hayes   Jane Lynce   Larry David
Kate Upton

Movie Story:
Moe, Larry, and Curly start out life at a childhood orphanage. As adults they inadvertently all meet up together again. They learn that the orphanage is struggling to remain open and so they hatch a plan to make a lot of money. They accidentally stumble into a murder plot and in a bazaar twist of fate get their own reality TV show.

300 Series Number:
The Three Stooges are trying to kill a man. He is hit by a bus and is in the hospital in Room <u>386</u>. That's right room 386.

He is not in room 227 or 717 or 586 or 619. He is in room <u>386</u>.

Movie Title: The Amazing Spider Man
Date Released: 7/4/2012
Date Viewed: ~12/4/2012

Major Stars:
Andrew Garfield
Emma Stone
Martin Sheen
Rhys Ifans
Sally Field

Movie Story:
Peter Parker is Spiderman. He was an outcast in high school and was raised by his Uncle Ben and Aunt May. This unusual circumstance occurred because he was abandoned by his parents as a boy. One day Peter discovers a briefcase that belonged to his father and he begins to put the pieces together as to why his parents left him. While on tour of Oscorp with fellow students he meets Dr. Curt Connors his father's former partner. Peter begins to suspect that Dr. Connors has stolen his father's work. Dr. Connors performs uncharted experiments on himself and becomes a huge mutant lizard. Spiderman and the lizard battle each other.

A Multiple Number 3 Scenario:
Young Peter Parker goes into the city to scope out where a scientific associate of his late father works. He is standing in the city street and behind him is a storefront that has a 3 on it. It is an address. It says <u>3</u> Columbus Circle.

Peter gets in on a tour of the building "Oscorp." The first room they walk into a man comes walking out of a glass door that has a <u>big number 3</u> on it. Unbelievable! The man is Dr. Connors who is the main scientist there.

While Peter Parker is still in the building he bumps into a deadly serious looking guy. A folder falls on the floor and Peter bends over to pick it up and he sees the double zeros crossed out on a form in the folder and that is the work that his late father had been working on. He follows this guy and the guy goes into a room whose <u>door is labeled L3</u>. That's right L3. He goes into this room and that is where he gets a spider on him.

In a later scene Dr. Connors decides to inject himself with the experimental DNA and he goes into <u>lab number 3</u>. It is the lab with the large number 3 on the sliding glass doors.

There is another Third Floor quote from a Buk book. The book is called "Pulp" and the line is from page 70. Check it out if you get a chance. Many people consider "Pulp" to be Buk's worst book so if you are new to Bukowski do not consider this book to be indicative of his other works. I just really like the line from page 70.

Movie Title: Total Recall
Date Released: 8/2/2012
Date Viewed: ~1/2/2013

Major Stars:
Colin Farrell
Kate Beckinsale
Bryan Cranston
Bokeem Woodbine
Bill Nighy

Movie Story:
Welcome to Rekall, the company that can turn your dreams into real memories. A factory worker named Douglas is bored with his monotonous life. Taking a mind-trip sounds like a great idea, almost a vacation. He would love to experience the life of a superspy. He decides to do the procedure but something goes terribly wrong and now he is a hunted man. He manages to escape capture with surprising skills he never knew he had. He teams up with rebel fighters to battle against Chancellor Cohaagen who has his mind set on global domination. Something is not quite right. Perhaps Douglas is not who he thinks he is. He eventually discovers his true identity and his full set of skills come into full use.

Third Floor Quote is Level 3 and many 3's:
Colin Farrell's character, Doug, arrives in the United Federation of Britain after there has been a terrorist attack for another day of work. An announcer over the intercom says, "Security elevated to <u>level 3.</u> Please remain in scanners until cleared."

Doug asks his coworker Harry who is played by, Bokeem Woodbine, what he knows about ReKall. He says, "Remember Travis from <u>shift 3,</u> went to Rekall for his bachelor party. Got himself lobotomized!"

Doug is training the new guy who looks like an Asian dude and he says to Doug, "Hey, you know your friend was wrong, by the way, about

211

Rekall." Doug says to him, "What, you done it?" The new guy says, "Heh, been <u>3 times</u> already."

In a later scene at night in a bar Doug and his work friend Harry leave and go outside and it's raining. Doug is standing there talking to Harry and there is a dark blue, big number 3 painted on the wall behind him. Why? Why? Why?

Kate Beckinsale's character called Lori is supposedly Doug's wife. Lori tries to kill Doug because it turns out that Doug is actually a top-flight intelligence agent. He narrowly escapes from Lori and she extremely quickly gets on the walkie-talkie and says, "<u>Team 3</u> break position. I need you on site now." Are you kidding me? Are you Fucking kidding me?

There is a car crash in these totally cool air / magnetically controlled cars. He, Doug, is being driven by Jessica Beil's character. They drop down to a lower level. A cop in a helicopter who is tracking them says to all police vehicles, "Suspect is headed to suspension <u>level 3</u>, repeat he has headed to suspension <u>3</u>." Holy Crap.

Towards the end of the movie Colin Farrell's character whose real name is Hauser, commandeers a helicopter and he flies to the location where all of the bad guys are about to launch a military operation from. The on board voice of the helicopter says, "<u>Bay 3</u> access granted."

As he makes his way on foot there is an announcement over the intercom by one of the military commanders and he is saying, "We are a go on code 3, 1, zero (<u>310</u>). Citizens of the colony are to be considered hostile,"

Ladies and gentlemen that is six mentions of number 3 in one movie! For me, the guy who is writing a book like this, it is a mother lode of 3's. What is the deal here with this movie? This is really unbelievable.

Movie Title: Tales of Ordinary Madness (Italian)
Date Released: 10/10/1981*
Date Viewed: ~6/15/2013

Major Stars:
Ben Gazzara
Ornella Muti
Susan Tyrrell
Tanya Lopert

Movie Story:
Poet / lecturer Charles Serking performs a reading. The next day he awakens and has to make his way back to L.A. When he gets home he interacts with his friends and neighbors but then meets the most beautiful woman he ever saw and enters into a dark and troubling relationship with her.

300 Series Number:
Bukowski's character lived in <u>Apt. 314</u>

The woman in this movie, Ornella Muti, is so beautiful it is astonishing. The scene where she stands with her naked backside exposed while standing over by the window is enough to make any man want to jump into the TV. She is extremely beautiful.

This movie is creepy. It didn't do well in the U.S. at all. Practically no one knows about this movie. Only serious fans of Charles Bukowski do. The movie did fairly well in France. This movie is strange and dark. This is not a good introduction to Bukowski at all. If you want to see Bukowski type movies watch Barfly and Factotum. There are also DVD's like "Born Into This" and the double DVD, "One Tough Mother" which, contains two of his public readings. It's in the DVD's in "One Tough Mother" where you get to see and become more familiar with the <u>real </u>Bukowski. After you have watched all of those you may be ready for Tales of Ordinary Madness.

Daniel McTeigue

Movie Title: Wild Target   (100)
Date Released: 11/5/2009
Date Viewed: ~7/11/2013

Major Stars:

Emily Blunt   Rupert Everett   Martin Freeman
Bill Nighy   Eileen Atkins
Rupert Grint (Harry Potter)

Movie Story:
Victor Maynard is an aging man who lives a solitary life and he just happens to be an assassin. He is known for his ruthless efficiency. His cold hearted routine is interrupted when he finds himself drawn to one of his victims. He decides to spare her life and unexpectedly acquires a young apprentice. Unaware of Victor's true vocation Rose and Tony tag along while he himself avoids being shot by his unhappy boss.

300 Series Number:
While Emily and Bill's characters are in the car together Bill says to her, "3rd street on the right."

When all 3 characters have to check into a hotel the killer (Bill) says to the clerk, "3 rooms please." The 3 of them argue.
Then the Hostess says, "why don't you settle this in 322. It's one of our cheapest."

I just found this movie while I was in the documentation process of writing this book. I saw that Emily Blunt was in the movie so I rented it and here is has a 300 series number in it! Ha Ha Haa!!!

Here's another Bukowski quote for you. This is from the book "South of No North." It's from page 123. Buk has just got done having sex with some hot little number and they're making plans about getting together again.

"Will you come see me again?" she asked
"Of course."
"You live upstairs?"
"Yes. 309. I can come see you or you can come see me."
"I'd rather you came to see me," she said.
"All right," I said. I got dressed, opened the door, closed the door, walked up the stairway, got in the elevator, and hit the 3 button. (12*)

Movie Title: G I Joe: Retaliation
Date Released: 3/29/2013
Date Viewed: ~7/31/2013

Major Stars:

Bruce Willis	Jonathan Pryce	D. J. Cotrona
Dwayne Johnson	Lee Byung-hun	Adrianne Palicki
Channing Tatum	Elodie Young	
Adrianne Palicki	Ray Stevenson	

Movie Story:
Due to some deception the G.I. Joes are framed for crimes against the country. The president has no choice but to terminate the G.I. Joe branch. The G.I. Joes refuse to take this demotion lightly and continue to fight their mortal enemy, Cobra. Even though they are dealing with threats from their own government they continue to uphold the high moral contract that they signed up for.

A Level 3 Quote:
In the beginning of the movie some G.I. Joes raid a building in Pakistan where the bad guys have a nuclear bomb. One of the G.I. Joes says, "Level 2 secure, moving on to <u>level 3</u>."

Movie Title: The Great Gatsby
Date Released:
Date Viewed: ~8/16/2013

Major Stars:

Leonardo DiCaprio

Toby McQuire

Carey Mulligan

Joel Edgerton

Adelaide Clemens

Elizabeth Debicki

Isla Fisher

Jason Clark

Amitabh Bachchan

Movie Story:

An adaptation of F. Scott Fitzgerald's Long Island set-novel, where midwesterner Nick Carraway is wowed by and lured into the fanciful world of his neighbor Jay Gatsby. It doesn't take long for Carraway to see the cracks in the veneer of Mr. Gatsby's world. The outlandish lifestyle and over indulgence of the great Gatsby is eventually the source of his undoing.

Third Floor Quote:

Someone at one of the amazing parties at the Great Gatsby mansion asks Toby McGuire's character, "Your face is familiar. Weren't you in the third division during the war"? The person asking is the Great Gatsby, played by Leonardo DiCaprio.

I admit this is a bit of a stretch for me to put this in there but it is another example of how the number 3 is used so often. There are countless other examples I've noticed over the years but I couldn't use them because I had to remain focused on the Third Floor. This is similar to Will Smith in "I Robot" with him being beat up in the 3rd grade.

Movie Title: R I P D
Date Released: 7/19/2013
Date Viewed: ~10/13/2013

Major Stars:

Jeff Bridges

Ryan Reynolds

Mary –Louise Parker

Stephanie Szostack

Movie Story:
You are not going to believe this but when people die they continue to live. A recently slain cop finds this out when he is appointed to the Rest in Peace Department which, is manned by un-dead police officers. While he is working he tries to find the man who murdered him. Based on the comic by Peter M. Lenkov.

Three more times Quote:
At the very end of the movie Ryan's character says, "53 more years huh"? Jeff Bridges character, Roy, says to Ryan Reynolds character, "Well, I still got some things to work on, hell, this is the third time I've been extended."

Movie Title: Monster's University
Date Released: 6/21/2013
Date Viewed: ~11/7/2013

Major Stars:

John Goodman	Peter Sohn	Julia Sweeney
Billy Crystal	Sean Hayes	Bonnie Hunt
Steve Buscemi	Dave Foley	Bill Hader
Helen Mirren	Charlie Day	John Krasinki
Joel Murray	Bobby Moynihan	

Movie Story:

In this movie we get to re-visit the wonderful characters of Mike and Sully. The story here covers the time of their college days at Monster's University. It's hard to believe but in their early days they weren't even friends.

A 300 Series Number and a Third Door Quote:

Billy Crystal's character, the little green guy, is at his new college and it is his first day. He goes to the front desk to get his room number assignment from the man behind the counter. The man, or should I say monster, says, "Wazowski, room 319. You know, your roommate is a scarer major too."

The young monsters are out at night and they are on the roof of the Monsters Incorporated building. They are looking at older professional scarers working on the scare floor. They are each calling out names of their favorite scarers. At one point John Goodman's character, the big blue guy says, "Ohh, third door from the end." Then Mike the little green guy says, "Carla Killer Claws Benitez."

So here we go folks. I am trying to put the finishing ends on my book here, but as I watch new movies I'm getting more and more new data. It's just unbelievable.

Special note: isn't it interesting to hear how similar, in general, that Wazowski's last name is similar to Bukowski's. The only thing different is the first three letters.

Movie Title: The Pacific Rim
Date Released: 7/12/2013
Date Viewed: ~11/15/2013

Major Stars:

Idris Elba	Burn Gorman	Robert Kazinsky
Ron Perlman	Rinko Kikuci	Larry Joe Campbell
Charlie Hunnam	Max Martini	
Charlie Day	Robert Maillet	

Movie Story:
Legions of monstrous creatures known as Kaiju start rising from the sea. Humanity fights back and millions of lives are lost and a tremendous amount of resources are consumed over many years. Massive robots called Jaeger's were invented by humanity. They are controlled simultaneously by two pilots whose minds are locked in a neural bridge. The Kaiju's continued to grow in size and complexity and the massive Jaeger's can barely fight them back. When humanity is on the verge of defeat two people are called on to pilot an old, nearly obsolete Jaeger. With the help of a plan devised by two mad scientist, humanity makes its last desperate attempt at annihilating the horrifying Kaiju.

Multiple Number 3's:
There are three Chinese brothers who are triplets and they are an extremely effective fighting team inside one of the Jeagers or fighters. There is a brief scene where they are playing basketball together and you can see a number 3 painted on a cargo vessel door.

A few minutes after that one of the main characters who plays an unruly son yells to his dog, "Max, come here." In a quick second up behind him you see a number 3 if you look over his left shoulder. Briefly after the dog runs to the guy you see a huge 3 painted on the wall. It's a white number 3 on a drab green wall.

There are numbers painted on walls all over the place in this movie. However there are two important scenes that take place in the Marshall's private room. The Marshall is a super intense black guy. When the Marshall has to tell the Japanese woman, Miss Mori that she can't participate in the attack, this occurs with big <u>number 3's</u> painted on both walls behind her.

In a different scene the Marshall goes back to his room. He is not feeling well and he is splashing water on his face from a sink. The big number <u>3's</u> are totally obvious on the walls.

There was an earlier scene in the movie whereby the bad news was that 3 workers died from working on the top of the new wall. The good news was that 3 new workers were needed.

Threes were absolutely everywhere in this movie.

Movie Title: Red 2
Date Released: 7/19/2013
Date Viewed: ~11/27/2013

Major Stars:

Bruce Willis	Catherine Zeta-Jones	Lee Byung-hun
John Malcovich	Anthony Hopkins	Titus Welliver
Helen Mirren	David Thewlis	Neal McDonough
Mary-Louise Parker		

Movie Story:
Frank Moses is a retired C.I.A. agent. He has to reunite his eclectic team of elite operatives. They have one more assignment and that is a global quest to track down and disarm a missing portable nuclear device.

A Number 3 Scenario:
Hon is Korean and he is the best contract killer in the world and he is out to kill Bruce Willis, John Malkovich, and Mary-Louise. A black dude who we see for the first time in the movie is leaning against the wall next to an elevator. We can see the #3 as plain as day.

Movie Title: Admission
Date Released: 3/22/2013
Date Viewed: ~ 12/23/2013

Major Stars:

Tina Fey	Ben Levin	Gloria Reuben	Lily Tomlin
Paul Rudd	Ann Harada	Wallace Shawn	

Movie Story:
Portia Nathan is a straightlaced Princeton University admissions officer. Portia is told by an old friend of hers that a student in his class may be the child that she had given up for adoption many years ago. She goes to see the young man and is told by her old friend that he is a very gifted child. Her friend John, suggests to her that she could get the gifted student named Jeremiah into Princeton. Portia has herself convinced that this boy may very well be her long lost son and she begins to bend the very strict rules of the admissions office.

300 Series Number:
Tina Fey's character, Portia, who works in the admission office, has her own office and it is <u>Room 310</u>. There is a scene when her boss comes to talk to her after everyone has found out that her boyfriend has dumped her and you can see her office number clearly.

Movie Title: Elysium
Date Released: 8/9/2013
Date Viewed: 12/21/2013

Major Stars:

Matt Damon

Alice Braga

Jodie Foster

Sharlto Copley

Jose Pablo Cantillo

Diego Luna

Wagner Moura

William Fichtner

Adrian Holmes

Movie Story:
Two classes of people exist on planet Earth in the year 2159. The very wealthy live on a pristine man made space station called Elysium. All of the rest of humanity live on an over populated ruined Earth. Jodie Foster plays a heartless government official who will stop at nothing to ensure that no unauthorized people land on Elysium. This fact doesn't stop black market entrepreneurs from trying to get people onto Elysium, largely for medical healing. One man named Max is poisoned in an industrial accident and the only chance of his survival is to make it on to Elysium. He becomes the central character in a far sweeping plot to bring healing to both worlds.

Third Floor Quote and 3's all over the place:
Matt Damon's character Max has to go to the hospital because some robot cops broke his arm. When he goes to the hospital he meets his childhood friend Frey who is a nurse. She is working on his arm when some other hospital staff person says, "Frey they need you up on the <u>Third Floor</u>. (HaHa HaHaHa HaHa HaHaHa aaahhh).

Jodie Foster's character, Secretary Rhodes, who is a top official, is hailed into a security situation where <u>three</u> unauthorized ships are trying to land on Elysium. There is a screen that says, ALERT LEVEL <u>3</u>, as she walks in the room.

A corporate scum bag who oversees the company where Max is injured severely is planning on flying up to Elysium via a small super fancy red aircraft but Max and some supposed bad guys want to capture him. The aircraft he flies in is labeled 3B.

Max and his friends are attacked while trying to capture John Carlyle, the corporate creep. They are confronted with a military flying machine. Max escapes the battle but is hunted. At one point he sees the vehicle above his head and you can see the numbers 302.

On a side note Jodie Foster's character shuts down all of the air space over LA., Bukowski's town.

When the military air ship crashes on Elysium with Max, Frey and her child onboard, a government helicopter which is flying above the scene says to the home base, "Two illegals heading north in zone 3." He is saying this in reference to Frey and her daughter as they are running on the ground. Two scientist on Elysium were about to suck the data out of Max's mind but he completely freaks out and breaks out of the shackles and nearly strangles one of the scientist to death but instead he asked the scientist,

"Where did they take the girls?"

The scientist responds, "The armory."

Max asks, "Where the fuck is that?"

The scientist says, "Level 3."

When one of the renegade soldiers leaves the room after the psycho leader soldier, Kruger, stabs Jodie Foster's character in the throat you can see a big #3 on the wall.

As all hell is breaking lose Max has to get to the armory. We see him go into an elevator and push the 3 button. You need to realize that the director of this movie purposely put that close up scene in this movie.

This movie absolutely cracked me up because I am literally in the final process of writing the book. I am doing a whole lot of copying and pasting in order to get all of the information in a smooth order. I was tired and looking forward to going upstairs to watch a movie. I have been looking forward to seeing Elysium because it looked really cool and here we go with a classic straight up Third Floor quote as well as a bunch of 3's everywhere. This mystery is blowing my mind.

Oh, *By The Way*, if you know the answer to the Third Floor mystery don't tell ANYBODY!!!. Seriously. If you and a few other people know the answer to this profound and mind staggering mystery, don't tell anybody. Please wait three full years from the year of publication of this book so that I can make some money. After all, I have been documenting this data for 20 plus years. This has taken a long time and it has taken close to a year and three quarters to put this whole thing together. Please don't blow it for me. Lay low for three years and then I guess you can reveal the answer.

One of Charles Bukowski's best poems is "Dinosauria, we." You have to read this poem and then compare it to Elysium. There are a lot of similarities between the two. I doubt those who made Elysium are unaware of "Dinosauria, we." I wouldn't doubt that they are fans of Bukowski's work.

Movie Title: Blue Jasmine
Date Released: 7/26/2013
Date Viewed: ~1/22/2014

Major Stars:

Cate Blanchett

Alec Baldwin

Sally Hawkins

Bobby Cannavale

Louis C.K.

Peter Sarsgaard

Andrew Dice Clay

Michael Stuhlbarg

Movie Story:

A wealthy woman who lives a comfortable life in New York city is forced to move out West to live with her sister after her husband is arrested for financial fraud. She fights hard to adapt to her life without money and it is indeed a great struggle.

300 Series Number:

Cate Blachett's character, Jasmine, arrives at her sisters house in San Francisco. The address is <u>305</u> S. Vanace. We get to see a close up of the <u>305</u> on the door. Jasmine calls her sister Ginger on the phone. "Hello Ginger, Yes, I'm here. I'm right in front of the place. <u>It is 305</u>."

In a later scene Ginger goes to get her kids from her ex-husband who name is Augie. Andrew Dice Clay plays Augie and him and the two boys come walking down the steps of a <u>3 story</u> wooden building. Nobody says Third Floor but you can see it.

Do you remember what other movie had an address and a close up of the number 305?

Movie Title: Bullet to the Head   (110)
Date Released: 2/1/2013
Date Viewed: ~2/3/2014

Major Stars:

Sylvester Stallone   Sarah Shahi
Jason Momoa   Sung Kang
Christian Slater
Adewale Akinnuoye-Agbaje

Movie Story:
A nearly unimaginable alliance is formed between an ice cold hit man and a top notch cop. Each man saw his partner killed and they are drawn together to bring down their common enemy.

Third Floor Quote:
Sylvester Stallone's character's name is Jimmy BoBo. Some creeps have double-crossed him. They've killed his partner and now they have his daughter. He has to go meet the bad guys in an old abandoned building to do an exchange. When he gets there and gets out of his car one of the bad guys says, "OK BoBo, up the stairs, <u>Third Floor</u>."

That bad guy just made my day.

Movie Title: Easy Money (Sweeden)   (111)
Date Released: 1/15/2010
Date Viewed: ~3/29/2014

Major Stars:

Joel Kinnaman	Matias Varela	Dragomir Mrsic
Lisa Henni	Mahmut Suvakci	Jones Danko
Lea Stoianov	Dejan Cuki	

Movie Story:

JW becomes a drug runner in order to maintain his double life. Jorge escapes prison and so is on the run from the police but also the Serbian Mafia. Mrado is a Serbian Mafia en- forcer who is on the hunt for Jorge. These three men's fates are all tied together as the story culminates into a crashing crescendo.

Third Floor and Series 300 Quote:

Two cab drivers are sitting in their own cabs parked next to each other discussing upcoming cab fares. They are both main characters and the cab driving thing is just a cover for their other illegal activities.

The cab driver says to his boss, "Malmvagen 98 in Sollentuna."
The boss says, "98?"
The driver says, "Third Floor."
The boss leans over and hands his employee and envelope and says, "Good Job."
The driver says, "Thanks, catch you later."

Towards the end of the movie a big cocaine deal is about to go down. The deal is going to happen in a loading dock area. A truck arrives on the scene and as it slowly drives by we can see a 334 reflected on a glass window.

Movie Title: Side Effects   (112)
Date Released: 2/8/2013
Date Viewed: ~4/17/2014

Major Stars:

Jude Law	Emily Rooney Mara
Catherine Zeta-Jones	Martin Channing Tatum
Polly Draper	Ann Dowd

Movie Story:
A woman turns to prescription medication as a way of handling her anxiety concerning her husband's upcoming release from prison. It would seem she is on medication but actually she is involved in a play of deception.

Series 300 Quote:
Close to the end of the movie the main character, Emily Taylor, played by Rooney Mara goes to see Dr. Banks, played by Jude Law. Dr. Banks and all of the other people involved with being deceived by her are there as well in the lobby. She is forced to take medicine as one of the conditions of her punishment. The address sign of Dr. Bank's office is 310-1E. Even though his office is on the ground floor it is still a 300 series number.

Movie Title: Bad Ass 2: Bad Asses   (113)
Date Released: 4/8/2014
Date Viewed: 6/11/2014

Major Stars:
Danny Glover
Danny Trejo
Andrew Divoff
Jacqueline Obradors

Movie Story:
An old Vietnam vet named Frank Vega runs an East LA community center where he trains young men to be boxers. He has a favorite boxer whom he trained and is ready for an important fight. Unfortunately he is involved with drugs and ends up dead. Frank's heart is broken and he vows revenge. An old friend of his Bernie, teams up with him as they go out into the mean streets looking for the man who murdered Frank's favorite pupil.

Third Floor Quote:
Frank and Bernie force some information out of a bad guy and they go to the location. It ends up being a frat party. They ask a young guy there, "We're looking for Hammer." The frat guy gets fresh and tells the old guys to get off the property. Bernie grabs his fingers and twists the young guy to the ground. The kid is in intense pain. Bernie says to him again, "Where's Hammer?" The frat guy says, "OK, OK, OK, KKKK He's, He's He's up stairs <u>Third Floor</u> Room 5!"

Movie Title: The Grand Budapest Hotel   (114)
Date Released: 4/8/2014
Date Viewed: 6/11/2014

Major Stars:

Ralph Fiennes	Jude Law
Tony Revolori	Ed Norton
F. Murray Abraham	Saoirse Ronan
Mathieu Amalric	J. Schwartzman
Adrien Brody	Tilda Swinton
Willem Dafoe	Bill Murray
Jeff Goldblum	Tom Wilkinson
Harvey Keitel	

Movie Story:

The Grand Budapest Hotel tells of a legendary concierge at a famous European hotel between the wars and his friendship with a young employee who becomes his trusted protégé. The young man is the new Lobby Boy. The story involves the theft and recovery of a priceless Renaissance painting, the battle for an enormous family fortune and the slow and then sudden upheavals that transformed Europe during the first half of the 20th century. Directed by Wes Anderson it is a pleasure to the eye.

Third Floor Quote:

Ralph Fiennes character "M. Gustave" is in prison unjustly. He is taken in by a group of four inmates. They tell him of their plan to escape. While they are escaping at night they have to descend a long ladder. As they are going down a random convict sees them. As they shout-whisper back and forth to this person you can see painted on the wall behind them "CELL BLOCK C <u>Floor 3</u>."

Owen Wilson playing Sr. Hotel Staff says to one of his co-workers as they are standing behind the main check-in counter, "Tell tactical logistics we're moving into a standard double on the <u>Third Floor</u>."

I can't say enough good things about this movie. It was as if each scene was an artwork unto itself. The framing of the scenes by Wes Anderson was a joy to watch. His use of color and lighting was incredible. Some scenes were so well done they made me laugh out loud. There is one scene were a car drives through a small European town at night with snow on the ground and every angle and nuance is perfect. Ralph Fiennes was perfect and the new guy on the scene Tony Revolori as Zero the Lobby Boy was fantastic. Wes Anderson co-wrote this movie with Hugo Guinnes so we can't forget him. They were inspired by the writing of Stefan Zweig. I also loved the music in this movie. It was very similar to the music from "The Fantastic Mr. Fox" also done by Wes Anderson. Sure enough the music was done by the same guy, one, Mr. Alexandre Desplat. I absolutely love the music this guy composes for the different scenes.

I have studied drumming for my whole life and I have to tell you that the snare work for the theme song in "The Fantastic Mr. Fox" was very interesting to me and I had real hard time tapping out that beat. Usually I can figure out any beat but that one had me stumped.

I think it is safe to say I am a real fan of Wes Anderson. I look forward to his next movie. I enjoyed the Grand Budapest Hotel so much that I bought it on pay per view. I am way too broke to do that sort of thing but the Grand Budapest Hotel is the sort of movie you can watch again and again.

I am so glad that my book has ended on such a wonderful movie.

The mystery continues…

Movie Title: It's Complicated   (RUSH Category)
Date Released: 12/25/2009
Date Viewed: ~5/25/2010

Major Stars:

Meryl Streep	Mary Kay Place	Zoe Kazan
Alec Baldwin	John Krasinski	Nora Dunn
Steve Martin	Rita Wilson	
Lake Bell	Alexandra Wentworth	

Movie Story:
Ten years after their divorce, Jane and Jake Adler unite for their son's college graduation and unexpectedly end up sleeping together. But Jake is married, and Jane is embarking on a new romance with her architect, Adam. Now, she has to sort out her life -- just when she thought she had it all figured out.

Special Category Quote:
When Meryl Streep goes to New York City she stays in the Park Regent Hotel. She stays in Room 2112. Is Meryl Streep the greatest actress ever? Uumm. YES!

That's right Room 2112. This is a special category section and the topic here is RUSH. You know......RUSH, the Rock Band.

If you don't know about it you have to go outside right now and buy the CD and listen to it over and over again. The album is called 2112. This is something that you have to do. Go. Go. Go.

If I haven't said this already I better say it now. Neil Peart is the best drummer who ever lived.

I really enjoyed the show FRINGE. I can't believe it ended after only three seasons. They played some fantastic music on that show. When I was a kid if I got sick I was taken to Abington Hospital. I grew up in Lasndale. Fringe mentioned both of these places in their shows. This really blew my mind. The Episode "Man From Other Side" opens with the RUSH song "Tom Sawyer." On a Season 2 Episode Agent Broyles, the super intense thin black guy sings "Low Spark of High Heeled Boys." In another show Walter, the mad Scientist is listening to YES. I noticed these things and they made my day.

CHAPTER TEN

THIS IS THE END,
OH BEAUTIFUL FRIEND

It is time to wrap this thing all together now. This Third Floor Movie Mystery is one strange phenomenon. I surely hope there isn't some drab explanation to this whole occurrence. I hope this book encourages many a discussion and brings forth all sorts of ideas. I am going to try hard to get my book into the hands of a few big time movie stars so that they themselves can ponder this conundrum. I also hope that if I do get this book into the hands of a few movie stars that they will then buy a few copies for their movie star friends and that way a bunch of the people who star in these movies will read about the Third Floor Movie Mystery with their own eyes. I hope, I hope, I hope.

As I look back over these particular stories of my life I am reminded of my hunger to live. I always had a desire to get into the thick of it. The thrill of intense athletics was very enticing. It was hard not to get involved once you had gotten a taste of it. I couldn't take the fear that maybe I was missing out on something. Some of the injuries I experienced in Ice Hockey were truly horrible. I have a few injuries from those days that have left lasting pain in my body. The amount of running we did in soccer practice in Junior High was barbaric. The football players who practiced close by even felt horrible for us. They would talk to us after practice and with looks of genuine concern on their faces. They would ask us, "Why do you guys have to run so much"?

I'll never forget the days of running like a bolt of lightning when I was on the track team. One day a few days before our first track meet we were given our uniforms. Uniforms? Little did we know that when you run sprints you wore virtually nothing. We all had to buy track spikes, which are lighter than a feather and have four very sharp spikes in the front part of your foot. We were each given "lighter than air" baggy silk shorts and a sleeveless shirt. These fabrics were so light that when you put these "clothes" on you felt virtually naked. When we got out to the track and ran some sprints I knew it then that I was ready for the Olympics. I felt like a God. I felt so in tune with my body it was exhilarating. The way that the spikes gripped the track was magical. My track mates and I looked at each other and couldn't believe this feeling of swiftness. The metal spikes bit into the soft and yet firm gravel of the track and propelled you forward like a rocket. We were the Purple and White Vikings of Penndale.

My time of playing Ice Hockey was the most important of all the sports I ever played. To be dressed in full Ice Hockey gear for the first time was to feel like a gladiator going to battle. You felt invincible to pain. You were covered from head to toe in a fortress. You almost felt sorry for the players on the opposing team of which you were going to enjoy slamming into the boards. When I could skate at a very high level of skill it was a joy to go flying down the ice during practice or in the games when you had the puck on your stick with opposing players struggling to catch you. The joy of scoring a goal in Ice Hockey is one of the most joy / adrenaline producing things that any sportsman / sportswoman can experience on this Earth. I was lucky to play alongside of all my teammates at both the High School and Men's league levels. To play in the Men's league was a real honor. Those guys and that level of play brought out the best in me.

As much as I loved being an athlete and being gifted with a trim, strong athletic body it was music and drumming that I loved the most. Many people may not believe that we live over and over again on this Earth. What I have read, studied, and learned has led me to be a believer in the knowledge that we live again and again. In this life I was meant to be a drummer. From the time I was a kid I was drawn to drumming and the flow of rhythm like it was the ether of my life. I am SURE that other people are born with urgings within them that draw them to things like guitar, violin, piano, painting, drawing, hunting, fishing, mothering, gardening, mechanics, computers, writing, athletics, etc., etc. We get the strong urges from our soul which lines up a general life path for us. I tried four times in my life to be a guitar player. About two years after Third Floor had broken up my old friend Phil saw me struggling on the guitar on one of my simple early lessons. I was trying like mad to hold my fingers in position to play a clean chord and it was torture. The guitar made me look like a total spaz. My friend Phil just casually said, "Dude, God never intended for you to be a guitar player." He said it with such self-confidence that it rung true. It made total sense to me but I stuck with the lessons for a few months but then naturally gave it up because it wasn't meant to be. I was meant to be a drummer and that is why my inner self drove me so strongly to that goal. When it came to the drums even as a young kid I made progress every time that I sat down to play in good ole Roslyn. How do you explain Mozart composing symphonies at age 4? He had been on Earth before composing symphonies!

I consider it to be an honor to have jammed with every musician I ever played with. Every bandmate I ever had I considered to be a good person. Believe me they weren't all Saints with their drinking and smoking and cursing habits. Some of the folks throughout the years liked to smoke some good pot to get in the mood for jamming. I enjoyed getting high. It was critical to expanding my mind so I could be creative. I had to come up with new drum tracks for song after song. You need to be very creative to survive something like that. Not everybody partook and that's okay too. That's the way it was in the 1980s! There was a whole lot of partying going on. It was a pleasure to be in those bands. It was a pleasure to be in a band and to feel the music grow in strength with each passing week and month. One of the fondest feelings is the stunned silence when the song ends at rehearsal and everyone knows to stay silent because the tape's rolling but once I hit the pause button all hell breaks loose to all of our collective disbelief that we just nailed the shit out of that song. A roar of joy, laughing, and high fives breaks the brief silence. Myself along with the members of Third Floor made some incredible music. We really did!

This whole Third Floor Movie Mystery is some business. I stumbled onto it only as a result of having Third Floor emblazoned across my brain, my heart, my soul. I'm so glad I got a list going and kept it going. It happened to be a good thing that as a senior pharmaceutical research technician, then many years later as a Scientist, I was required to write down everything I did while at work. That discipline bode well for me when it came to writing down every movie I saw that had a Third Floor in it. I have loved movies so strongly throughout my life. I have loved movies going all the way back to the days of "Love Bug" and "Born Free." My cousins and I used to be dropped off at the Keswick Theater in Jenkintown, Pennsylvania back in the late 1960s and early 1970s when I was 8,9,10. I loved how movies took me away from my drab existence. Thank God for cinema. Thank God that there is a steady stream of people who are so inspired by movies that they want to make movies when they grow up. We all need movies for a brief escape from the difficulties of our long lives in this labor intensive world. Every once in a while a movie will come along that captures the imagination of the whole world. You have to admit that when this occurs it is something really special.

As you know I swore I was going to keep this book a lighthearted affair and I am. But I saw a show a few nights ago in the ongoing series called Ancient Aliens. What a fantastic show. The episode was all about the number three. It talked about the power of the number three going back to Biblical times. It was a very interesting show. I myself have read things over the years concerning the number three. Multiples of the number three are present in every facet of our modern society. Here are just a few examples: 3 strikes and you're out, 9 innings in a baseball game, a dozen eggs, 12 months in the year, a bushel is $12 \times 12 = 144$. The Father, The Son, The Holy Spirit. Small, medium, large. Here is an interesting metaphysical quote from the show.

"Three is the great mystery that comes from the one. Three is the power of transformation."

Perhaps we as people who live on the Earth have the number three deeply embedded into our psyches and we are barely aware of it when we write it down. Perhaps many of these writers are even unaware they are writing Third Floor when they do. They may be on autopilot when they express the number 3 in one of its forms. Who knows?

I hope people get a kick out of my book. I'm sure that the people who read this book will forever be observant of this mystery. I hope people are curious to hear some Third Floor music too so I'm going to post some on Facebook and YouTube and on a Third Floor Movie Mystery Book specific website. (www.thirdfloormm.com) I am sure there are many movies that I have not seen that have a Third Floor quote or 300 series number in them. I hope the mysterious forces that help guide this realm keep the Third Floor Movie Mystery going even after my book comes out. Now that the Third Floor Movie Mystery has been exposed will it remain the same or has it now been altered as a result of being observed. I may have caused an extreme change to the mystery by bringing it forth in such a public manner.

I certainly hope it continues.

ABOUT THE AUTHOR

"The Third Floor Movie Mystery" is the first book of new author Daniel H. McTeigue, pronounced Mc Teg. Dan was compelled to write this book as a result of discovering the constant prevalence of the phrase "Third Floor" in movies. As the list grew to close 100 movies he knew he had to share his findings. He is a college graduate with a Bachelor Degree in Science with a major in Biology from Gwynedd Mercy University. Dan has always been very active in sports. While in Jr. High School he was on Championship winning Track and Soccer teams. While in High School he played Ice Hockey and won another Championship. However, the author's deepest love is drumming. He was consumed with drumming all of his young life. His goal was nothing short of becoming world famous. All through his 20's he was is Rock bands. The last and best band he was ever in was "Third Floor." Throughout his whole life he has always loved movies. With the invention of the VCR and subsequent video stores Dan was in movie heaven. He was also an avid skier, particularly all through the 1990's.